UNIQUE EATS AND EATERIES

OF

THE PEOPLE AND STORIES BEHIND THE FOOD

MATT STEWART

Library of Congress Control Number: 2022937106

ISBN: 9781681064109

Design by Jill Halpin

Photos by author unless otherwise noted.

Printed in the United States of America
22 23 24 25 26   5 4 3 2 1

We (the publisher and the author) have done our best to provide the most accurate
information available when this book was completed. However, we make no warranty,
guarantee, or promise about the accuracy, completeness, or currency of the information
provided, and we expressly disclaim all warranties, express or implied. Please note that
attractions, company names, addresses, websites, and phone numbers are subject to change
or closure, and this is outside of our control. We are not responsible for any loss, damage,
injury, or inconvenience that may occur due to the use of this book. When exploring new
destinations, please do your homework before you go. You are responsible for your own
safety and health when using this book.

DEDICATION

To Chrissy,

For your love and support; for inspiring others while fighting cancer;
and for exploring local eateries with me on our fun date nights.

Chicken N Pickle
Courtesy Chicken N Pickle

CONTENTS

INTRODUCTION

Kansas City is known as the king of barbecue. With more than 100 barbecue restaurants in the metro, you'd be hard-pressed to find a bad one. But we're not just about smoked meats and sauce. Talented, award-winning chefs from all over the world have opened restaurants here, and they have found success feeding this town new and exciting flavors.

Selecting the most unique restaurants proved to be quite a challenge. There are so many to choose from! First, I established certain criteria: the restaurant needed to be locally owned, serve unique food, offer a dining experience different from other restaurants, and have a historical or fascinating backstory. I will admit, some great restaurants were left off this list. I made tough choices and picked restaurants I thought best represented the culinary experience of Kansas City. Every restaurant is located within the metro area—some on the Missouri side, some on the Kansas side. To keep this project manageable, I left out eateries from nearby towns like Weston, Excelsior Springs, and Leavenworth. While they are home to some *very* unique restaurants with a ton of history, I didn't have space to include them. Some of your favorite restaurants might not be in this book. I'm sure I missed a couple that deserved consideration. However, the ones I have chosen represent a mix of cultures, recipes, and stories that set them apart from the rest.

What makes me a culinary expert? I have spent nearly two decades working as a broadcast journalist in Kansas City, and my daily reports have taken me to many of these restaurants. I didn't pick them based on taste (though they all serve wonderfully delicious food!). I picked them based on their story. Within these pages, you'll meet the two godfathers of Kansas City barbecue, Arthur Bryant and Ollie Gates, who popularized both burnt ends and all things smoked. I'll introduce you to the great-great-great-grandson of a whiskey distiller who revived the family business in an old brewery; an ice cream shop that only hires people with special needs; the burger stand/former flea market where a serial killer once worked; and a diner where you can buy a meal for the homeless. These stories and others will help you better appreciate the food you're eating—and the people who made it for you. My hope is that you use this book as a scavenger hunt map and mark off each restaurant as you visit, expanding your palate along the way.

I want to thank everyone who supported me on this project. If fellow author Anne Kniggendorf hadn't suggested my name to Josh Stevens from Reedy Press, I never would've been asked to write this. Thanks to everyone at Reedy Press who polished my writing and made this book happen. Thanks to my PR friends who sent me information and pictures from many of these restaurants. And I want to thank my wife Chrissy; my kids Jackson, Alex, and Maddy; and my friends for waiting patiently as I took pictures of their food before they could eat it. Most of all, thank YOU for reading this. I hope you discover some great restaurants you never knew existed, and I hope that you enjoy the food as much as I did!

UNIQUE EATS AND EATERIES

OF

KANSAS CITY

AFFÄRE

An authentically German affair

For more than 200-years, Martin Heuser's family has been in the cooking business. Their restaurant in Bonn, Germany, called *Im Steinhaus*, sits inside a stone building dating back to the 1400s. Martin's descendants passed down their love of cooking to him, and he grew up learning the family trade. But after a while, he yearned to spread his wings.

After finishing chef training in Bonn, Martin moved to Stockholm, Sweden, to work under world-renowned chef Werner Voegeli. After returning to Germany, he worked at several Michelin Star restaurants and earned the title of Master Chef, the highest diploma in this field. He met his future wife, Katrin, at an Irish bar in Germany where she worked. She'd lived in Hong Kong and loved to travel, so, after getting married, they decided to move to Vancouver so Martin could work at a French restaurant.

Wait, French? Yes, the man can cook anything.

While in Canada, Katrin studied wine in Vancouver and Calgary and earned the sommelier diploma through the International Sommelier Guild. At the same time, Martin competed in the Culinary Olympics for Team Alberta and earned a bronze medal. Now he was an Olympic-medal-winning chef. The opportunity to be an executive chef in Kansas City led Martin and Katrin to move here in 2007. Five years later, they decided to open their own restaurant. Martin would cook, and Katrin would handle the wine pairings. They found a great space in the Crossroads District and in 2012, they opened Affäre.

The couple wanted to bring Germany to the Midwest, so they designed their restaurant with that in mind. Guests can sit outside in a courtyard that features lush plants, artwork, and a

Left: *Venison Steak Truffle demi glaze with vegetables.*

Center: *Affäre Owners Martin and Katrin Heuser.*

Right: *The lights outside welcome you inside for a modern German dining experience.*
All images courtesy of Affäre

fireplace. They can sit inside in a cozy, darkened room where a painted table features a display of desserts. Speaking of desserts, Martin's specialty is Black Forest Cake with dark chocolate cherry filling soaked in kirsch. That dish originated in his hometown. He also makes holiday cookies using the same recipes as the German monks in medieval times (as well as recipes passed down from Katrin's great-grandmother).

As for the main course, they serve authentically German artisan brats and sauerkraut along with European delicacies like Wachteln (quail), gebratene Entenbrust (duck), and Hirschrücken unter Kräuterkruste (venison). And don't forget the German beer on draft!

Martin and Katrin love sharing their countries tastes and continue to offer farm-to-table fare with a seriously German twist.

1911 Main St., Kansas City, MO, 816-298-6182
affarekc.com

Affäre in German means Affair. They named it that because when you eat their food, they want you to feel the passion that went into making it for you.

JESS AND JIM'S STEAKHOUSE

How an article in a nudie magazine changed everything

Playboy once called Jess and Jim's the "finest steak restaurant in the world." In honor of that title, the restaurant offered customers a 25-ounce cut of beef they called the "Playboy Steak."

This world-renowned steakhouse started as a bar and grill. In 1938, Jess Kincaid and Jim Wright opened a small eatery on the corner of 135th and Holmes in Martin City. Soon after, Jess got married and sold his shares to Jim. Instead of changing the name, Jim honored their close friendship by continuing to give Jess top billing. Ten years later, Jim asked his cousin R. C. Van Noy to work for him. Jim grilled the steaks while R. C. ran the front of the house. Business grew. But in 1957, an F5 tornado blew through town and destroyed the restaurant. It was closed that night so no one was hurt, but the building was gone—and Jim didn't have insurance. Fortunately, R. C. owned another building nearby, so they reopened Jess and Jim's there.

Then in 1972, *Playboy* ranked Jess and Jim's as one of the best steakhouses in the country. Crowds suddenly came down in droves. The surge in demand forced Jim and R. C. to expand the building twice, going from 100 seats to 250 seats total. In 1977, Jim's health started to deteriorate, so he left the business to R. C. However, R. C. owned another restaurant nearby that specialized in fried chicken. His three sons ran that business while he took over Jess

---

While known for steaks today, Jess and Jim's used to be known as the best place in the metro area to go for frog legs!

Left: *An F5 tornado destroyed the original building. This is what it looks like today.*

Bottom center: *Owners Mike and Debbie Van Noy.*

Top right: *A perfectly cooked steak.*

Bottom right: Their steakburgers are rated by some as the best in KC. *All images courtesy Jess and Jim's Steakhouse*

and Jim's. In 2002, R. C. passed. His son Mike Van Noy took over Jess and Jim's while another son, David, continued running the chicken eatery, R. C.'s Restaurant and Lounge.

Mike's kids and grandkids help him run the place today. Mike hand-cuts the beef every day while his son makes homemade garlic toast and his daughter makes the carrot cake with caramel cheese frosting. Besides their delicious, award-winning steaks, they've also earned great reviews for their steak-burgers, twice-baked potatoes, and pickled beets. And they continue to rack up the awards from national publications like *Men's Journal, Esquire,* and *Travel + Leisure.*

517 E 135th St., Kansas City, MO, 816-941-9499
jessandjims.com

CHRISTY'S TASTY QUEEN

Taking pork tenderloin to the next level

It's one of Eric Stonestreet's favorite places to eat.

The Emmy-award-winning actor, known for his role as Cam on *Modern Family*, was born and raised in Kansas City, Kansas. His family still lives in the area. Whenever he visits, he'll often stop by Christy's Tasty Queen to grab one of their famous pork tenderloin sandwiches.

But 30 years before Lowell and Marla Christy started selling tasty pork tenderloin out of this small building, it was a drive-in called Henry's Burgers. The original owner opened the hamburger stand in 1957 to keep his son busy and out of trouble. The Christy's neighbor, Bob Carter, later bought it to help pay for his kids' college education and changed the name to Carter's Tasty Queen. When his final child graduated in 1983, he sold it to the Christys, who wanted to own a restaurant closer to home.

At the time, Lowell and Marla owned Hughes Drive-In in Windsor, Missouri, a two-hour drive from KCK. Marla's parents ran the place during the week while Lowell and Marla went there on weekends. The previous owner had given them her pork tenderloin recipe, and everyone there loved it. It called for two small tenderloins in a bun, so the Christys served it that way. But when they opened their KCK restaurant, they changed it up. Lowell is a meat cutter by trade and decided to go bigger. He cuts the pork tenderloins every morning, and his son runs them through the tenderizer. They're then sliced into thinner steaks so the employees can dip them in flour and batter and cover them with homemade breading. They are then fried and served on a bun with all the fixings. The sandwich has gained a reputation as one of, if not the, best pork tenderloins in the metro area.

Left: *An employees breads massive pork tenderloins daily to keep them fresh.*

Top right: *The 1950s-style façade invites customers to step back into the past.*

Right: *A selfie actor Eric Stonestreet took with the staff hangs near the front counter. He loves the pork tenderloin and often visits when he's in town.*

During the first 25 years of business, their business grew steadily. Then in 2008, the *Kansas City Star* published a feature on their pork tenderloin in the Food section. That's when business exploded. Later that day, cars parked helter-skelter as a line of people waiting to try it stretched down the street for blocks. Since then, many visit daily wanting their fix of fresh pork tenderloin. Make sure you get there early, or you might find yourself standing in line.

Unless you're Eric Stonestreet. He gets to cut to the front.

1405 S 55th St., Kansas City, KS, 913-287-2800

The Christys used to ship tenderloins all over the country, from New York to Wisconsin to Hawaii! They don't ship anymore, though, because it's too expensive and time-consuming.

BREW LAB

Sharing the art of homemade brewing

They hatched the idea over beer. The accountant, the realtor, the IT guy, and the college professor. Four friends with different jobs all sharing the same interest: beer. Specifically, a love for brewing beer at home.

Wanting to help other home brewers, Clay Johnston, Justin Waters, Kevin Combs, and Josh Turpin combined forces in 2013 to open a store that sold home-brewing supplies. Things like grains, hops, yeast, tubes, tanks, and other gadgets. They also offered classes to teach budding brewers the art of making stouts, ales, and lagers. Within a few years they'd outgrown their space and decided to move into a bigger building. They also decided to retool to become one of the few craft breweries in Kansas City with a full-scale kitchen so they could offer food along with their homemade beers.

What's fun about Brew Lab is you can make your own beer concoction from scratch. They'll help you do it, whether you come with your own recipe or create a new one. Keep in mind, it's a process. From start to finish, it takes weeks to brew a batch of beer. And when it's ready, you'll go back and bottle it before taking it home to drink and share with others.

If you're not into making beer, you can still enjoy the craft brews they make in-house along with the food they serve from

Brew Lab has been known to sell beer made by its customers. If they like it and choose to put your beer on their tap, then you'll really have bragging rights on your friends.

Top left: *After brewing your own beer, you can bottle it there.*

Bottom left: *Take the beer home with you, if you'd like.*

Bottom center: *Grab a flight and try all the different styles of beer on tap.*

Top right: *Nachos go great with a craft beer.*

Bottom right: *The original founders of Brew Lab gather before opening their doors.*
All images courtesy Brew Lab

their kitchen: tastes like truffle fries, street tacos, wraps, and burgers. While the menu is simple, they elevate it so people will continue to come back.

When the COVID-19 pandemic hit in 2020, the owners feared it might sink them. But thinking outside the box, they set up a series of outdoor concerts with local bands. People listened from their cars and balconies and supported them by ordering food and growlers of beer to go. It kept them afloat. Today, they are thriving, giving beer lovers a place to learn how beer is made and the opportunity to make it themselves.

7925 Marty St., Overland Park, KS, 913-400-2343
brewlabkc.com

ANDRÉ'S CONFISERIE SUISSE

Swiss chocolates from heaven

André Bollier's idea to bring Swiss chocolates to Kansas City didn't pay off right away. André was a pastry chef in his hometown of Basel, Switzerland. He and his wife Elsbeth wanted to open their own candy shop there, but it cost too much to do in their home country. André called his brother, who was living in Kansas City, and asked for advice. His brother told him there were no luxury European chocolate confectionery shops in the Midwest and encouraged him to move to Kansas City to open one.

He and Elsbeth went all in. In 1955, they moved their family to the United States and opened a chocolate and pastry shop on Main Street. Using only the highest-quality ingredients and old-world techniques, the Bollier's made and sold luxury Swiss chocolates and pastries.

But no one bought them.

Kansas City residents didn't understand what André was trying to do. They didn't want to pay higher prices for sweets. Facing financial ruin, the Bolliers needed to do something to get people inside their store. First, they added traditional Swiss baked goods to the menu like Danish, croissants, and coffee cakes. Then, they began offering lunch. They opened a small tea room and served traditional Swiss dishes like quiche lorraine and chicken and mushroom vol au vent. They knew if people came in to eat, they would buy chocolates and pastries on their way out.

It worked.

After 10 years of hard work, the Bolliers developed a reputation for making great Swiss food. Customers love the traditional Swiss pastries like the Napoleon, a three-layer, crisp, puffed pastry, and the Matterhorn, pieces of chocolate cake mixed

Top left: *Their decadent sandwiches feature flaky buns.*

Bottom left: *André's has been making Swiss chocolates out of this building since 1955.*

Center: *Many publications rank André's chocolates as some of the best in Kansas City.*

Top right: *The coffee, cake, and macaroons are also fantastic.*

Bottom right: *Founders Andre and Elsbeth Bollier. All images courtesy of André's Confiserie Suisse*

with buttercream and covered in chocolate fondant. As for the chocolates, André's uses the Swiss method of conching, where cocoa butter and chocolate are evenly mixed to create smooth, creamy candies. It gives the chocolate a distinct caramel taste.

Many questioned André along the way. Why didn't he move his family to a European city so his business could grow faster? But he always believed Kansas City was the perfect place to introduce Swiss cuisine. For three generations his family has reaped the rewards of this decision as customers continue to enjoy being transported to Switzerland.

5018 Main St., Kansas City, MO, 816-561-3440
andreschocolates.com

> André's best seller is chocolate-covered almonds. Of the 45,000 pounds of chocolate they make each year, more than half is used to cover the almonds.

LENEXA PUBLIC MARKET

Sharing serving space to test treats

She took a risk and it paid off.

Katie Liu-Sung always dreamed of opening a Taiwanese restaurant in Kansas City. Born in Taiwan, she moved to the Midwest for college and missed the street food of her youth. But when it came time to open her own eatery, she worried about buying a building and then not being able to pay back tens of thousands of dollars in loans. To minimize the risk, she instead decided to rent out space inside the brand-new Lenexa Public Market. She called her concept Chewology and sold Taiwanese street food and pan-fried dumplings. Her restaurant became so popular that after four years she had raised enough money to move out into her own building in Westport.

That's the goal of the Lenexa Public Market—to be an incubator for small businesses. Before building a brand-new City Hall on Lenexa's west side, city manager Eric Wade visited a public market in Milwaukee and fell in love with the concept. By providing an 11,000-square-foot space for small businesses to grow, it allows entrepreneurs to test their concepts without investing their life savings. It also provides an inviting place for the community to gather and connect around food, coffee, and retail—all while supporting local business owners. At any one time, 8 to 10 small businesses rent stalls to sell their goods. They control their hours, menu, and staffing. While restaurants can rent a space that comes with a kitchen, there's also a test kitchen upstairs where chefs can prepare their food before selling it from their stalls.

The cuisine varies depending on who is renting the space. Visitors have eaten everything from Pakistani to Mexican to West African food. One Mexican food stand serves breakfast burritos that were named the best in Kansas City by *Food and*

Top left: *The Public Market is connected to Lenexa City Hall. Courtesy Randy Braley Photography*

Bottom left: *A test kitchen allows chefs—and the public—to cook up new recipes. Courtesy Paul Versluis*

Center: *Chewology owner Katie Liu-Sung found so much success, she moved into her own space in Westport. Courtesy Chewology*

Top right: *Up to ten small businesses can set up shop inside the Public Market. Courtesy Bill Harrison*

Bottom right: *Butterfield's Bakery rented one of the few kitchens available. Other vendors set up their businesses in smaller stalls. Courtesy Bill Harrison*

Wine magazine. One chef offers mouthwatering butter chicken customers rave about. And the owner of a bakery started in the Market as a pop-up selling macarons with unique flavors, including boozy versions made with local spirits.

By the time you read this, there might be different chefs cooking up different foods. They all hope to find the same success as Katie. But no matter who is cooking up what, the Lenexa Public Market will always be a place for aspiring chefs to test their recipes on the public.

8750 Penrose Ln., Lenexa, KS, 913-477-7516
lenexapublicmarket.com

If you visit on Tuesday or Saturday you can walk outside and buy fresh produce and crafts at the local Farmers Market. They set it up in a nearby parking garage.

CUPINI'S

Making fresh noodles daily

He's made the longest noodle in the world and sent a meatball into space. He's also filmed a show for the Food Network with celebrity chef Guy Fieri. Eddie Cupini is always up for an adventure, especially when it promotes the great tastes at his Westport Italian restaurant. Ironically, he never wanted to get into the restaurant business in the first place—he once told a friend to shoot him if he ever did. And yet, fate had other plans.

Eddie's father, Franco, raised his boys on fresh Italian cooking. A graduate of the Culinary School of Rome, Franco's talents led him to cook for the President of Italy. But when his brother opened an Italian restaurant in St. Louis in 1968, Franco moved his family overseas to help. He taught Eddie how to make fresh pasta so he could help in the kitchen, but Eddie had other ideas. He joined the Navy and left home. After his tour of duty, Eddie returned to the only thing he knew—Italian food. He wanted to open an import business, but St. Louis already had a ton of them. Kansas City had one. So, Eddie moved across the state and began selling Italian goods to Kansas City restaurants. When one owner asked him to make fresh pasta, he did. They loved it, and the demand for his noodles soared. He couldn't handle all the orders himself, so he asked his dad to help. Franco moved to Kansas City, and soon after, they opened Cupini's.

> **Wanting to expand into the hair salon next door, Eddie intentionally cooked garlic in the basement every day because he knew the owner hated the smell. It worked! The owner quickly moved out and Eddie snatched up the space.**

Left: *From pasta to delicacies, you can get all kinds of Italian tastes at Cupini's.*

Top right: *All the pasta is homemade.*

Bottom right: *Owners Eddie and Franco Cupini. All images courtesy Eddie Cupini*

Since opening in 2003, they've racked up a bunch of accolades. Zagat once rated it one of the best Italian restaurants in the country. They make everything fresh every day, including rolling and cutting the pasta. The sauce comes from tomatoes canned within hours of being pulled from the vine. They also offer an assortment of desserts like tera miso and a variety of cellos—limoncello, orangecello, and blueberrycello, to name a few.

Their small, brick building features pictures of Eddie's family all over the walls. They show memorable moments like the time they broke the Guinness World Record for making the world's longest noodle. Or the time they glued a meatball to a weather balloon and sent it 63,000 feet into the air. But Eddie says the best thing about his restaurant is that they offer fresh Italian food at an affordable price. While many Italian restaurants charge $20 a plate or more, Cupini's charges half that. It's a deli, really, and he hopes to continue serving delicious, homemade pasta for many years to come.

1809 Westport Rd., Kansas City, MO, 816-753-7662
cupinis.com

NEIGHBORHOOD CAFÉ

A cinnamon roll with every meal

Everyone loves free food, especially when it satisfies your sweet tooth, and that's one of the big draws at the Neighborhood Café. Every time you eat there, you get a free cinnamon roll.

This tradition dates back to 1995, when Sue Meador opened up Sue's Kitchen where the Neighborhood Café sits today. She would occasionally offer her customers a free cinnamon roll, and they were so good that demand for them took off. Soon she began offering them free with every meal. When Neighbor's Café took over the space in 2001, they asked for Sue's cinnamon roll recipe and continued to give them out free—but in 2011, they went out of business. In stepped Tony Olson, Bob Baker, and Ben Wine, three friends who grew up eating at Neighbor's Café and loved the free cinnamon roll tradition. They teamed up to buy the restaurant and rebranded it Neighborhood Café.

This small-town diner is something out of *The Andy Griffith Show* and sits in an old brick building full of history. Built in the early 1900s, it was one of the first strip malls in downtown Lee's Summit and once housed a wagon repair shop, a shoe repair shop, a welfare office, and a grocery store. But the restaurants there haven't had a great track record. In 1951, Brown's Steakhouse opened—and closed. After that came, in order, Kozy Korner Café,

> Besides cinnamon rolls, there is one other staple on the menu: Liver and Onions. Many who try it are surprised at how good it tastes, and the owners are constantly surprised by how many people order it.

Left: *The egg sandwich is always a big hit.*

Top center: *Many restaurants have tried—and failed—in this same building.*

Bottom center: *Owners Kelly and Tony Olson, Ben Wine and Bob Baker.*

Top right: *Neighborhood Café is best known for their large portions.*

Bottom right: *Every customer gets a free cinnamon roll. All images courtesy Neighborhood Café*

Chuck Wagon, Linda's Restaurant & Steakhouse, Ida's Place, Ford's Family Restaurant, Thompson Restaurant, Sue's Kitchen, Neighbor's Café, and now Neighborhood Café.

Tony, Bob, and Ben are trying to prove they can succeed where others have failed. All their food is made homestyle. With most of their customers having come here for years, it's hard to change the menu. Every time they remove something, the customers keep ordering it anyway. And the cooks still make it. The one thing that will never go off the menu is the cinnamon rolls. They give away around 1,500 a day, helping the Neighborhood Café prosper in a place where others have failed.

104 SE Third St., Lee's Summit, MO, 816-524-4545
neighborhoodcafe.com

THE GOLDEN OX

Birthplace of the Kansas City Strip

Kansas City's nickname is Cowtown, and there's a good reason for that.

In 1871, they built stockyards at the confluence of the Kansas and Missouri Rivers to make it easier for ranchers to unload their livestock. The Kansas City Stockyard Company formed and built an exchange to determine the price of meat to be sold to the processing plants. The area exploded as close to two million cattle passed through the Stockyards every year.

Not happy with the dining choices in the West Bottoms (which is what they called the area), Jay Dillingham, president of the Stockyards, decided to open a fancy new restaurant. In 1949, he introduced the Golden Ox on the first floor of the Livestock Exchange Building. He decorated it with unique light fixtures and carpet adorned with cattle brands. Plush leather seats and dark rooms created an upscale vibe. To attract customers, his chefs invented a new cut of beef called the Kansas City Strip. It was a delicious, savory meat from the shorter side of the beef loin. Jay's insistence that they only serve the highest-quality beef attracted many to dine at the Golden Ox. But two years after opening, tragedy struck. The Great Flood of 1951 forced them to close when 30 inches of rain flooded the Stockyards. After drying out, they reopened and continued to have great success.

Business, though, began to dwindle. In 1991, the Stockyards closed for good, and the West Bottoms cleared out. Concerts at nearby Kemper Arena still attracted large crowds to the area, but then the city built a new downtown arena in 2007. In 2014, the city's oldest steakhouse closed for good. Or so many thought. Four years later, new investors reopened the restaurant, and while the pandemic

Top left: *Founder Jay Dillingham. Courtesy John Dillingham*

Bottom left: *The surf and turf. Courtesy The Golden Ox*

Center: *The Prime Rib cooked to perfection. Courtesy The Golden Ox*

Top right: *Being so close to the original stockyards, they are expected to serve the highest-quality steaks. Courtesy The Golden Ox*

Bottom right: *The Golden Ox still sits in the original Livestock Exchange Building. Courtesy The Golden Ox*

forced them to pause for a short while, they are back open and excited to welcome both the regulars and new customers alike.

Much of the décor and ambiance from 1949 remains. The beef tastes the same, as they serve only the finest cuts of meat. While most of their cuts are in the $30 to $80 range, their 56-ounce ribeye goes for $132 (though it does serve 2-3 people). But that's the price of business when you go back in time to relive the days when the Stockyards ruled the city and The Golden Ox was the place to get a steak.

1600 Genessee St., Kansas City, MO, 816-842-8846
goldenoxkc.com

The Golden Ox only serves dinner, so the new owners opened The Ox Café & Bakery next door inside the same livestock exchange building. You can go there for breakfast and lunch.

FANNIE'S WEST AFRICAN CUISINE

How a civil war survivor built a one-of-a-kind business

When Fannie Gibson first opened her restaurant in Kansas City's urban core, it was, to her knowledge, the only one that offered West African cuisine. Jollof rice. Egusi soup. Puff puffs. Staples to those who live in West Africa. Many West African transplants in Kansas City gravitated to her restaurant to enjoy the taste of home.

Fannie grew up in Liberia during a time of civil unrest. She was born in 1988. In 1989, one of Africa's bloodiest civil wars began. More than 200,000 Liberians were killed over a 14-year period, and more than one million families, including Fannie's, were displaced. Her grandmother lived in Kansas City and helped Fannie and her family escape from Liberia to Ghana. Once there, they applied to the refugee resettlement program, and US officials allowed them to move to Kansas City to live with Fannie's grandmother.

Fannie was 16 when her family arrived in Kansas City. She graduated high school and tried to become a nurse, but when she became pregnant, she dropped out. Wanting to provide for her growing family, she decided to give the restaurant business a try. For years she'd been cooking West African food for family and

> Goat and fish are the main staples in West Africa, not chicken and beef. The ingredients needed to make the food served at Fannie's are hard to find in Kansas City, so she gets weekly shipments from an African company in Chicago.

Left: *Cooking and serving the entire fish is a part of Fannie's West African culture.*

Top center: *Owner Fannie Gibson.*

Bottom center: *Sometimes Fannie cooks up something unique not on the menu like this dish of fried sweet potatoes, greens/leaves, and rice.*

Top right: *The puff puff is deep-fried dough with a doughnut-type taste.*

Bottom right: *Rice is a staple in West African cuisine. All images courtesy Fannie Gibson*

friends using recipes her grandmother taught her. She added her own twists and began posting pictures on social media. Her fan base grew as more people tried her food. They encouraged her to open a restaurant, and in 2016, she did. She found a place in the urban core that offered cheap rent and spent two years getting the place ready. When she finally opened, large crowds showed up and continued to come back.

Her food is unlike any you'll find in Kansas City. You can order a whole red snapper, mackerel, Plantains, kala with pepper sauce, or fufu with okra butter. Not sure what any of that is? Just ask! Fannie will proudly explain what's included in each dish. And bring your patience. Everything is made from scratch, so it takes time to make each dish. That's the West African way—cook slowly. This food takes Fannie back to her childhood, and it brings her joy to share part of her country's culture with others. She hopes to expand in the future to give even more people a taste of her homeland.

4105 Troost Ave., Kansas City, MO, 816-832-8454
fanniescuisine.com

TOM'S TOWN

Honoring a crime boss and his love of spirits

During Prohibition, Tom Prendergast ran this town. Despite the fact alcohol was illegal, the liquor-company-owner-turned-corrupt-political-boss used a large network of underground tunnels to move his spirits from one speakeasy to another. The police never busted him because he paid them off. Money, jazz, and booze flowed in the open under his watch, causing some to call Kansas City the "Paris of the Plains." When someone asked Tom why he ignored Prohibition, he simply said, "The people are thirsty."

Today, the people are still thirsty. Wanting to feed that thirst, Kansas City natives David Epstein and Steve Revare decided to open a distillery in Kansas City and name it after this iconic Kansas City legend. The childhood friends and budding entrepreneurs built their distillery in a 100-year-old building just blocks from where Tom Prendergast once kept his office. You can still see the char marks on the posts where a fire in the 1930s destroyed the first floor, which at the time housed a candy company. The stamped tin ceiling saved the building, and it is still there today. That, along with 1920s-era chandeliers and round marble tables, gives the place a speakeasy vibe.

Through a large glass window you can see the distilling equipment, and if you look up you'll notice a column going through the ceiling. The vodka column was almost five feet too

> On Wednesdays you can volunteer to bottle and label the alcohol at Tom's Town. In return, they will feed you and send you home with a free bottle of booze.

Left: *Tom's Town makes their own bourbon, vodka, and gin. Courtesy Tom's Town*

Top right: *Owners Steve Revare and David Epstein. Courtesy Tom's Town*

Bottom right: *The Bourbon Burger is one of many meals you can order with your drinks.*

tall, so they cut a hole in the ceiling to make room for it. Speaking of vodka, in 2017, *USA Today* named Tom's Town the Best Craft Vodka Distillery. They also make two types of gin and two types of bourbon, and they sell their craft spirits all over the country.

As for food, David and Steve hired a talented chef and gave her the freedom to make whatever dishes she desired. Her signature Bourbon sliders, crab toast, and charcuterie board are fan favorites. But the main event is the fun mixed drinks. For instance, the Tom Prendergast is double-oaked bourbon with smoked cinnamon agave. The Frozen Prohibition Punch includes apple brandy, gin, and pineapple juice. And the Pinky Blitz is a mix of vodka with blood orange, ginger shrub, and ginger beer. Every drink is named after something from the Prohibition era, and you'll be grateful Prohibition is over when you try their tasty drinks.

1701 Main St., Kansas City, MO, 816-541-2400
toms-town.com

THIRD STREET SOCIAL

Where being loud is encouraged

The name "Social" fits. Nearly 100 years before a restaurant opened here on Third Street, Harry Truman stood in the same spot to announce his candidacy for Eastern judge of Jackson County. Running on a platform of improving roads and "a day's pay for a day's work," Truman asked 600 fellow war veterans to vote for him. Then they went inside and watched wrestling, boxing, singers, dancers, and comedians as they talked and smoked free cigars.

The tradition of being social here continues at this downtown Lee's Summit restaurant. When Andy Lock and Domhnall Malloy first saw the unique brick building, they knew it would be the perfect spot for their new concept. They wanted a lively bar-centered restaurant that served comfort food and where people could relax and chat with friends. But before renovating this old brick building, they needed approval from the Historical Preservation Office. The original Memorial Hall, where Truman announced his candidacy for public office for the first time, burned to the ground in the 1940s. Sherwood Manufacturing rebuilt it on the original foundation and made pipe nipples here. Then in 1950, local benefactor Joseph Arnold bought the building and donated it to the city, and city leaders turned it into a community center.

When renovating this building, Andy and Domhnall took great pains to preserve the original brick and metal trusses inside, giving it a throwback feel. They also modeled it after upscale Chicago restaurants, installing plush round booths, a mosaic tile

> **Andy Lock is the father of Drew Lock, an All-SEC quarterback who played at Mizzou and was drafted by the Denver Broncos in the second round of the 2019 draft.**

Top left: *Owners Domhnall Malloy and Andy Lock also partner in several other restaurants in the metro. Courtesy Third Street Social*

Bottom left: *Their fried chicken is among the most popular menu items.*

Top right: *You can top off your meal with an oatmeal pie.*

Bottom right: *The layout inside encourages people to talk to one another.*

floor, and brightly colored lights for a modern vibe. They also added an outdoor patio with fire pits and yard games so customers could drink with friends after their meal.

Speaking of meals, the menu is inspired by Southern fusion. A favorite appetizer is the fried brussels sprouts and cauliflower. The fried chicken has a thin, crispy coating, and if you're feeling adventurous, you can get it Nashville hot. Many also love the mac and cheese with gouda and pimento. As for dessert, their best seller is the oatmeal pie cookie, which is much bigger than a Little Debbie.

Andy and Domhnall own several restaurants in the metro area, and while they all serve delicious food, Third Street Social in Lee's Summit is the most unique. Surrounded by history, customers are encouraged to make new memories through conversation.

123 SE Third St., Lee's Summit, MO, 816-384-2123
thirdstreetsocial.com

FRITZ'S RAILROAD RESTAURANT

A different way of delivering food

Choo-choo! At Fritz's, waiters don't bring your food. A train does. This unique food-delivery system is the brainchild of Fritz Kropf. Born in 1921, Fritz grew up in the restaurant industry. His father, John, opened a cook-to-order hamburger joint in Kansas City, Kansas, called John's Place, where he seared grilled onions into the meat and served the burgers on toasted buns. Fritz worked for his dad through high school and then decided to enlist in the military.

In 1940, Fritz joined the Navy and was stationed aboard the USS *San Francisco*, docked in Pearl Harbor the morning the Japanese attacked. Fritz survived the onslaught of bombs that fell on the US naval fleet, and he served bravely in the Pacific Theater until 1943. He was transferred to Great Britain, but appendicitis kept him from taking part in the invasion of Normandy. During the war, he served as a driver for aviator Charles Lindbergh and helped German scientists defect to America. In 1946, he left the military and returned home. But instead of re-joining his dad, he began working at a petroleum refinery.

> When a customer first called Fred's "Skat Kat" a train, he hated it. But then customers started bringing in railroad memorabilia to decorate the restaurant. Fritz gave in, and this railroad novelty is a big reason why the restaurant has been so successful.

Top left: *The breakfast sandwich includes hashbrowns, eggs, sausage, and cheese.*

Bottom left: *The original Fritz's. The other two are at Crown Center and Shawnee.*

Center: *Founder Fritz Kopf and his "Skat Kat" system. Courtesy Fritz's*

Top right: *You can get a train engineers hat with your order.*

Bottom right: *The delivery train as it looks today.*

Fritz met Virginia and after they married, he decided to return to his roots. The Kropf's opened two 1950s-style drive-in diners using his father's hamburger recipe. Due to a labor shortage, he struggled to find good workers. It was a constant headache. To fix this problem, Fritz invented a unique solution: the "Skat Kat." Customers would order their food by phone at their table. The cook would then put their food on a tray connected to a small vehicle on a track. It would then roll above the customer's heads and stop at their table with their food. It worked perfectly! The Skat Kat saved Fritz money on labor. It eventually evolved into a train, and today that is what Fritz's is best known for.

Fritz's five children grew up working at the restaurant, and in the mid-1980s, his youngest son Fred took over the family business. Today, Fred continues the tradition of delivering meals by train at three different Fritz's locations. While the train gets people in the door, it's the tasty food that keeps them coming back for more.

250 N 18th St., Kansas City, KS, 913-281-2777
fritzskc.com

COURTHOUSE EXCHANGE

An underground grill haunted by the original owner

Joseph Poggenpohl loves the Courthouse Exchange so much he refuses to leave—even though he died more than 100 years ago.

It was 1899 when Joseph and his son, Joseph Jr., started serving fine wine, liquor, cigars, and food from their saloon in downtown Independence. But in 1908, Joseph Jr. died, and two years later, Joseph Sr. died. At least one of them has been haunting this establishment ever since—even though it's no longer at its original location.

In 1975, the original Courthouse Exchange burned to the ground. Bill and Shirley Bailey, the owners at that time, reopened it in an underground cavern nearby. They built a bar and continued to sell burgers. Then in the 1990s, the Baileys retired and sold the establishment to Ken and Cindy McLain, who have preserved this piece of Independence history.

Rock walls, a wooden bar, and antique fixtures give the underground tavern a cozy feel. Many come for the great-tasting food. Their pork tenderloin has won awards, and the burgers and fried chicken are made from scratch. But the food's not the only draw—many also visit for the ghosts. Who are these spirits? One employee swears she's seen the ghost of Joseph Poggenpohl

> **Mediums who've visited Courthouse Exchange say many of the ghosts are trapped, reliving the last day of their life over and over again like the movie _Groundhog Day_.**

Top left: *The restaurant is in a stone cellar, and there are reports of ghosts haunting the place.*

Bottom left: *If you are too scared to eat inside, take your chicken wrap outside to the patio. Courtesy Courthouse Exchange*

Right: *Original owners Joseph Poggenpohl and his son, Joseph Jr. Courtesy Courthouse Exchange*

walking and staring at her several times. A little girl ghost named Emily likes to strategically leave dimes in places where she hangs out. Some kids have gone to the bathroom and returned to tell their parents that they played with "a girl named Emily in the bathroom." The employees have seen lights turn on and doors open on their own. One said she was pinched in an empty closet. During ghost tours, they've smelled rose water and cigar smoke. And they believe the third floor is home to a dark presence that does not want them up there. Why so many ghosts? They believe it's because downtown Independence was a hotbed for outlaws and the site of gunfights during the Wild West days, making it a place where many people died violent deaths.

If you don't like ghosts, visit during the day for the food. If you do, visit on the third Saturday night of each month to take part in a ghost tour. Either way, this underground haunt will make an impression on you.

113 W Lexington Ave., Independence, MO, 816-252-0344
courthouseexchange.com

WESTPORT FLEA MARKET

A swap shop turned burger joint

They call it "The Flea," and it serves one of the best burgers in town.

Mel Kelb opened it back in 1981 as an antidote to the stuffiness of the Plaza. He wanted a fun place for common folks, so he bought a former flea market in Westport. He resurrected the bazaar and added burgers and a bar. Many flocked to eat here before visiting the vendors who rented space inside to sell their wares.

In the late 1980s, the place became famous for its connection to a serial killer. Robert Berdella sold odd things in a stall he called "Bob's Bizarre Bazaar." In his spare time, he tortured and killed people. Between 1984 and 1987, "The Kansas City Butcher" (as he was called) murdered six young men in the Hyde Park area. He was eventually caught and spent the rest of his life in prison, dying in 1992 of a heart attack inside his prison cell.

"The Flea" overcame that bad PR and thrived for two decades. But in 2006, Hooters approached Mel about buying the space. They wanted to tear it down and build a new restaurant in its place. Mel agreed and signed the contract. When local businessman and Westport Flea Market fan Joe Zwillenberg heard about it, he reached out to Mel and offered to buy it. Mel said no. Joe was insistent. He called every day and begged, but it was too late. Hooters sent a bulldozer to the parking lot. Lucky for Joe, Kansas City leaders stepped in and stopped the building from being demolished, and Mel agreed to sell the restaurant to Joe.

Eating here is a fun experience. Everyone is greeted by an "Orderologist" who screams your order to the chef standing six feet away. Try the hamburger. It's been rated as among the best in Kansas City. And note that they don't take credit cards—just cash. There's an ATM nearby if you need to make a withdrawal. Drink

Left: *Owner Jeff Zwillenberg.*

Top right: *Their burgers have won numerous awards.*

Bottom center: *Despite a steady supply of beef, sometimes it's hard to keep up with demand.*

Bottom right: *Make sure you top off your burger with fresh lettuce and tomato. All images courtesy Westport Flea Market*

specialists will visit your table to take your drink order. And when you leave, you can take your picture with the odd Burger-mobile outside. It's just as it sounds—a car in the shape of a burger.

As for the flea market, it's still there—kind of. They don't sell knickknacks anymore, but the metal cage is filled with odd items as a reminder of this restaurant's history . . . one they continue to build on every day.

817 Westport Rd., Kansas City, MO, 816-931-1986
westportfleamarket.com

If you're really hungry, try the 5-Patty Challenge: when you eat a five-patty burger in less than 30 minutes, your meal is free and you get your picture on the wall.

THE ANTLER ROOM

"I don't know what I'm eating, but it's the best thing ever!"

It's a good thing Nick Goellner ended up hating politics. Otherwise, he might be running for office rather than running his own kitchen.

The Stillwell, Kansas, native graduated from the University of Kansas with a degree in political science but quickly became disillusioned after a short stint in politics. Wanting to do something completely different, he followed his sister to the French Culinary School in New York. He loved it. After graduation, he honed his culinary skills on a cruise ship and at fine dining restaurants in New York, Chesapeake Bay, and Kansas City. While working at The Reiger in downtown KC (a now-closed restaurant Al Capone used to frequent), Nick met his future wife, Leslie Newsam, who at the time was the general manager. They became engaged and moved to San Francisco. They then went to Copenhagen, Denmark, so Nick could work at Noma, the most famous restaurant in the world. After six months there, they returned to Kansas City to open their own place.

They found a small office building on Hospital Hill and opened The Antler Room in 2016. Why name it The Antler Room? Because it started with A, antlers were trendy at the time, and it referenced an old Prohibition-era speakeasy called the Antlers Club that allowed booze, gambling, and jazz. That's the attitude they adopted—to do whatever they wanted with the food.

While their first menu reflected a Mediterranean influence, it has since branched off into other international cuisine. They serve dishes like okonmyaki, cocoa rigatoni, and fried soft-shell crab. Every few weeks Nick replaces several dishes with something new. He uses unusual spices and tries to avoid salt, fat, and sugar. Instead

Left: *The menu is unique and changes all the time.*

Top center: *They serve smaller portions, and each dish explodes with flavor.*

Bottom center: *It's a small space so they offer outside dining on nice nights to feed more people.*

Top right: *Owners Leslie Newsam and Nick Goellner.*

Bottom right: *Antlers decorate the top of the shelf behind the bar. All images courtesy The Antler Room*

of serving massive portions, he offers small plates so customers leave satisfied but still craving more.

Since opening, The Antler Room has won numerous awards, including Best Chef in Kansas City and Top 100 wine bars in the country. Nick and Leslie believe it's because they were one of the first to serve the type of upscale cuisine you typically find at a five-star restaurant on the coast. As Leslie's grandfather said after eating their food for the first time, "It woke up my taste buds! I don't know what I'm eating, but it's the best thing ever!"

2506 Holmes St., Kansas City, MO, 816-605-1967
theantlerroomkc.com

Most of the woodwork in the restaurant—the bar, host stand, and tables—was built by Nick and Leslie's dads. Leslie's mom made the curtains, and Nick's sister is their pastry chef, making it a true family affair.

WOODYARD BAR-B-QUE

How a wood company put KC BBQ on the map

When it comes to making great-tasting barbecue, it's all about the wood. The type of wood determines the flavor. Frank Schloegel III's wood yard in Merriam sells all kinds: hickory, oak, cherry, apple, peach, pear, Osage orange, and pinion. Frank III, though, prefers pecan because it gives the meat he smokes at his restaurant next door a mellower flavor.

Frank III's grandfather, a German immigrant, started the Southside Coal and Wood Company in 1912, when coal was king. When he died in 1948, his son Frank Jr. moved the business from Westport to Merriam and transitioned to selling wood. As a marketing tool, Frank Jr. used a Hasty Bake Oven to teach wealthy white men how to smoke meat, which at the time was a Black man's game. Frank Jr. smoked ribs because they were cheap, and he gave them away to customers on weekends. One day a man by the name of Ollie Gates stopped by to buy wood for his new barbecue joint. Impressed, he used Frank Jr.'s wood at all of his Gates restaurants for the next five decades.

But Frank Jr. never opened his own barbecue restaurant—his son did. Frank Jr. taught Frank III how to smoke meat, and when he took over the wood yard he started catering on the side. Everyone loved Frank III's barbecue, and he credits the wood. He typically smokes with oak and hickory, but he prefers pecan when it's in stock. Encouraged by friends and family to open a restaurant,

> Woodyard prides itself on being the most dog-friendly barbecue restaurant in town. After lunch, Fido can work off the meal inside a fenced-in Woofyard, their on-site dog park.

Top left: *Chicken wings join a slab of meat inside the pit. Courtesy Woodyard Bar-B-Que*

Bottom left: *The restaurant sits next door to the original wood yard, where they still sell wood.*

Top right: *Founder Frank Schloegel III. Courtesy Woodyard Bar-B-Que*

Bottom right: *Chicken, pork, beef: they smoke it all. Courtesy Woodyard Bar-B-Que*

he partnered up with Ciaran Molloy, who runs the restaurant, and Frank III recruited family members to create new recipes and rubs. They smoke all kinds of meat daily in a massive stone pit with four ovens, burning wood from Frank III's wood yard next door.

After opening Woodyard Bar-B-Que in 2005, Frank III's friend STRETCH, who owns Grinders, came to eat and loved the food. He encouraged legendary chef Guy Fieri to take his show *Diners, Drive-Ins and Dives* to Woodyard, and then other celebrity chefs like Anthony Bourdain and Andrew Zimmern followed. The national exposure brought them instant success, and now those who want to taste true wood-fired barbecue come here.

3001 Merriam Ln., Merriam, KS, 913-362-8000
woodyardbbq.com

NEW THEATRE & RESTAURANT

Front row seats to dinner and a show

For 50 years they've entertained hundreds of thousands of people, feeding them dinner before treating them to a show. When they first opened, they didn't call it a dinner theater for fear people would think it too stuffy. Instead, they called it a playhouse.

Dennis Hennessy and Richard Carrothers got into the theater business after graduating from UMKC. In the late 1960s, they directed and produced shows for the Resident Theatre at the Jewish Community Center. But dinner theaters were popping up all over the country, and Dennis and Richard wanted to be a part of this new fad. They borrowed tens of thousands of dollars from family and friends, and in 1972, they transformed an old laundromat near the Country Club Plaza into Tiffany's Attic Dinner Playhouse. Their first show was Neil Simon's *Last of the Red Hot Lovers*, featuring a young actress by the name of Morgan Fairchild. They sold out. In fact, so many people wanted tickets they found themselves booked five months in advance. Their sudden success led them to open a second dinner theater in 1973 in an old movie house at 75th and Washington. They called it the Waldo Astoria. It, too, opened to sold-out crowds. Both Dennis and Richard reveled in their success while movie and television actors like Don

New Theatre is the largest and most successful dinner theater in the country. They produce five shows and average more than a quarter-million visitors every year.

Left: *The newly renovated theater offers a great view no matter where you sit.*
Courtesy Kent Jewett

Center: *Owners Dennis Hennessy and Richard Carrothers. Courtesy New Theatre & Restaurant*

Right: *The desserts are delectable, but they cost extra. Courtesy New Theatre & Restaurant*

Knotts, Marion Ross, and Jamie Farr came to Kansas City to star in their productions.

Full of confidence, Dennis and Richard tried their hands at movies. They moved to Hollywood, produced some films, and returned in the late 1980s with cash and dreams of opening a bigger dinner theater. They closed Tiffany's Attic and the Waldo Astoria, and in 1992, they opened their "New Theatre" in Overland Park. The 617-seat theater has a revolving stage, an orchestra pit, computer-controlled lighting, and a state-of-the-art kitchen. In 2015, they spent half-a-million dollars to renovate it, adding four-million LED lights.

The food is one of the stars of the show. Guests walk through a buffet and fill their plates with offerings like Santa Maria steak, whiskey chicken, extra creamy garlic roasted mashers, and baked ziti rigate. For an extra charge, you can get a cheesecake, pie, or cobbler for dessert. This dinner-and-a-show experience is why the New Theatre & Restaurant continues to thrive today.

9929 Foster, Overland Park, KS, 913-649-7469
newtheatre.com

FARINA/EXTRA VIRGIN

The psychology of fine dining

He's recognized as the best chef in Kansas City, and his modern Italian restaurants offer tastes you won't find anywhere else, like squid pasta, clam toast, and grilled octopus.

His name is Michael Smith, and he was the first Kansas City executive chef to ever win the James Beard Award, given to the best culinary artists in the country. That was back in 1999 when he worked at the only five-star restaurant in town, The American Restaurant. He quickly gained a reputation for breathing new life into a stale menu, offering fresh, simple, unfussy American fare. He then left to co-found Forty Sardines, which received a nomination by the James Beard Foundation for "Best New Restaurant." Wanting his own place, he opened Michael Smith Restaurant at 19th and Main in the fledgling Crossroads Arts District but closed that in 2019 to open up Farina, right down the block and across the alley from his other acclaimed restaurant, Extra Virgin.

Farina means flour in Italian, and he chose that name to highlight the homemade pasta he makes. Every noodle in every dish is made from scratch, and the types of pasta he offers range from potato gnocchi to penne rigate to cheese-filled caramelle to squid ink orecchiette. For those who like their meat red, Michael cooks pork roast, short ribs, and ribeye over a wood fire.

The highlight of Farina is the raw bar. You can try freshly shucked oysters, octopus, or salmon roe. Oh, and don't forget the wine. Michael's wife, Nancy Smith—who is also his partner, general manager, and sommelier—oversees an extensive, well-curated selection of wine from all over the world. Her talents have garnered her the Award of Excellence from *Wine Spectator* since 2008.

Michael's love for cooking comes from his mother, who used to manage restaurants. After graduating college with a degree

Top left: *Owners Michael and Nancy Smith. Courtesy Ron Berg*

Bottom left: *Squid ink orecchiette. Courtesy Farina*

Bottom center: *Both Farina and Extra Virgin offer an elegant dining experience. Courtesy Farina*

Top right: *Anyone up for oysters? Michael is a master at seafood. Courtesy Jenny Wheat*

Bottom right: *Besides seafood, you can also order pork and beef cooked over a wood fire. Courtesy Farina*

in Psychology, Michael decided to become a chef. He wanted to learn from the best, so he apprenticed in both Nice, France, and at Charlie Trotters in Chicago before cementing his reputation in Kansas City. It's a well-deserved reputation, but don't assume that it's gone to his head. In fact, Michael is really easy to talk to. Don't be surprised if he stops by your table to engage in conversation, as he loves seeing customers enjoy his food.

19 W 19th St., Kansas City, MO, 816-768-8800
farinakc.com

Michael's restaurant next door, Extra Virgin, served Spanish tapas for years, but in 2021, Michael switched the menu to a new concept and now serves fresh Mediterranean food.

CREATIVE CULTURE

How an eight-year-old's bold idea became a reality

Crafts and milkshakes. The brainchild of a child.

While eight-year-old Annie Upp vacationed in Florida with her mother Dell Ann in 2018, they stopped at an ice cream shop that offered creative ice cream milkshakes. While enjoying this sweet treat, Annie suggested they open a store in Kansas City and serve similar milkshakes—while also offering crafts.

The idea wasn't so far-fetched. Dell Ann owned a craft shop in Manhattan, Kansas, where parents and kids painted pottery. Annie loved the place. But Dell Ann and her former husband, Kelly, also owned a party-planning business. Since most of their business was in Kansas City, they sold the craft store and moved. Annie missed doing crafts with her mom. While eating that milkshake in Florida, she convinced Dell Ann to open another craft store—that served milkshakes, too. Dell Ann loved the idea, and together they started a new business.

First, they spent hours in the kitchen experimenting with different milkshake recipes. The goal was to make them over-the-top. The S'mores shake overflows with marshmallows, graham crackers, chocolate, and a cinnamon roll. The Strawberry Cheesecake is topped with an actual slice of cheesecake and pop tart. The Local Love has a cupcake and cookie on top and changes colors based on the sports season: red for the Chiefs, blue for the Royals. They also offer seasonal milkshakes like pumpkin and peppermint.

Next, they needed a good location. They found a spot in Westport and signed the lease in February of 2020, but a month later, COVID hit. Not wanting to shut down, they offered take-

Left: *There are all kinds of crafts you can do when you visit.*

Center: *The milkshakes are over the top and come in all kinds of flavors.*

Right: *Owner Dell Ann Upp was inspired by her daughter, Anne, to open this craft-milkshake concept. All images courtesy Creative Culture*

home art kits and milkshakes to-go. The public supported them, and eventually they reopened. Families can now paint pottery, grow plants, and do other projects. Everything is do-it-yourself. And it's not just for the kids. Adults can also bring in alcohol and host a DIY party in the back.

Dell Ann and Annie have big plans. They've opened a second milkshake-craft studio in Leawood and a third one in Portland, Oregon. They hope to open many more throughout the country. Annie trains the employees on how to make the milkshakes. Dell Ann brings in new craft ideas. Together, this mother-daughter duo is shaking up the creative culture in Kansas City and beyond.

207 Westport Rd., Kansas City, MO, 816-569-3445
creativeculturekc.com

In fall 2021, a speaker wire caught fire and the inside of their Westport studio was destroyed. They lost most of their supplies and shut down for months. Insurance covered the damage, and they have since renovated and reopened.

THE PEANUT

Winging it since 1933

The oldest dive bar in Kansas City is proud of two things: they've held a liquor license longer than any other establishment in the city, and they serve the best wings in town.

The Peanut opened in 1933 after Prohibition ended. The owners were among the first to apply for the right to serve liquor, and they've been serving drinks ever since. In fact, they sell more liquor at The Peanut than any other small bar in Kansas City! But it took years to become the must-stop destination it is today.

The origin of The Peanut's name is unknown, although a small apartment complex right behind it was called the Peanuts. The bar served only alcohol until the 1940s, when the owners built a barbecue pit out back. In the late 1970s, the food went away, and they once again became a gin joint. It wasn't until the 1980s that The Peanut became the iconic eatery it is today.

Rich Kenny bought The Peanut in 1981. He wanted to offer food, so he asked his friend's ex-wife Melinda, who worked as a caterer, to build the menu. She went with buffalo wings and BLTs and nailed both recipes on her first try. Many publications rate her buffalo wings as the best in Kansas City, and for that, she credits her unique bleu cheese, which is more frosting than dressing. As for the BLT, it's inspired by her father, who ate tomato, onion, and cheese sandwiches in the summer. She added bacon and a few more ingredients, and now it's one of her most requested items.

> The original Peanut's dining room is only 450 square feet and can seat 50. If it's busy, the wait might be long—but if you stay, you'll be rewarded for your patience.

Top left: *The buffalo wings are rated by many as the best in Kansas City.*

Bottom left: *It's tight inside so be prepared to wait during the busy hours.*

Top right: *The Peanut used to be a gin joint before becoming the iconic restaurant it is today.*

Bottom right: *The BLT, inspired by Melinda's father, is one of the most requested items on the menu.*

Over the years, Melinda has tried offering new foods but has since given up because her customers keep ordering wings and BLTs.

Rich fell in love with her food and then fell in love with her. They married in 1983 and together built The Peanut into what it is today. In 2007, Rich passed away from pancreatic cancer, but Melinda carries on. She has allowed others to franchise The Peanut name and recipes, but she still owns two locations: the original on Main and The Peanut downtown.

Melinda is proud of what she and Rich built. Some customers come to The Peanut straight from the airport with bags in hand. Others travel to Kansas City specifically to try her food. She soldiers on, offering an experience no other bar can replicate.

5000 Main St., Kansas City, MO, 816-753-9499
peanutkc.com

DONUTOLOGY

The science of creating your perfect donut

It's gone where no donut has ever gone before: space.

The Space Donut at Donutology is the result of an experiment conducted by founder Andrew Cameron. He wondered what would happen if he sent a donut into earth's upper atmosphere. So, with childlike wonder, he glued a cake donut with sprinkles to a weather balloon and launched it from Marceline, Missouri, the childhood home of Walt Disney. He covered the donut with silicone to protect it from the harsh cold and 100-mph winds. It slowly floated 97,000 feet up into the air and there it stayed for nearly four hours—when the balloon finally popped. The donut then fell at terminal velocity and landed 253 miles away in a farm field in Illinois. A GPS chip helped Andrew find his Space Donut in a tree, unscathed. He now proudly displays his pride and joy behind glass inside his store.

Andrew loved donuts as a little kid and wanted to make them his career. Early on, he franchised several Daylight Donuts stores in the Kansas City area but dreamed of letting customers make their own donuts. In 2016, he sold his Daylight Donuts shops and opened Donutology in Westport, inside a 1940s-era Art Deco-inspired building once owned by Tower Cleaners. He transformed it into a donut laboratory. When customers walk in, they watch as employees knead the dough, cut it into mini donuts, and dip them

> Andrew partnered up with local shirt maker Charlie Hustle to create Donutology-themed T-shirts that are so popular people will come in to buy shirts instead of donuts.

Top left: *This iconic building used to be a laundromat.*

Bottom left: *The staff makes the donuts right in front of you.*

Bottom center: *You can personalize your donut order, choosing from 40,000 different combinations.*

Top right: *The donut that went to space is on display and not edible, so eat one of these instead.*

Bottom right: *Owner Andrew Cameron. All images courtesy Donutology*

in hot oil. Customers then discover their "donut gene" by choosing from more than 40,000 different drizzles and donut topping combinations. Bacon, Fruity Pebbles, and S'mores are just a few of his favorites. If you want a more traditional donut, they also make glazed, apple fritters, and cinnamon rolls.

Andrew makes his donuts from scratch every morning using fresh ingredients from local companies. And he loves to experiment. His job reminds him of his childhood, when he would eat donuts with his dad. Now he gets to sell that same happiness to others.

1009 Westport Rd., Kansas City, MO, 816-298-5222
donutology.com

JOE'S KANSAS CITY

Award-winning BBQ inside a gas station

If you want to eat some of the best barbecue in the country, you'll have to stand in line outside a gas station to get it. Joe's Kansas City is nestled inside a former convenience store in Kansas City, Kansas, where drivers still pull up to fill their tanks with gas—and their stomachs with barbecue.

Jeff and Joy Stehney began selling their award-winning barbecue there in August of 1996. But before diving into the restaurant business, they tested the taste of their smoked meats on the barbecue contest circuit. They attended their first competition in 1990 and competed under the name "Slaughterhouse Five." The judges loved their recipes, and the Stehney's went on to win 22 national championships. One of their competitors, Joe Don Davidson, owned a business called Oklahoma Joe's Smoker Company out of Stillwater, Oklahoma. He, too, had won a lot of awards for his barbecue and befriended the Stehney's. He proposed they go into the restaurant business together. In 1996, they opened their first Oklahoma Joe's restaurant in Stillwater. Later that same year, they opened a second Oklahoma Joe's inside the KCK gas station. The popularity of their barbecue exploded as people waited outside in line for up to an hour just to order a meal.

Eventually, the Stehney's and Davidson parted ways. Davidson continued to operate Oklahoma Joe's restaurants down south while the Stehney's bought out the Kansas City location and changed the name to Joe's Kansas City. Despite the name change, the recipes have stayed the same. They've won national accolades for their ribs and fries. The *New York Post* named Joe's the best barbecue restaurant in the nation. And visitors from all 50 states have traveled to KCK to try their meats. The most popular sandwich on the menu is the Z Man, a combination of provolone cheese,

Top: *The original restaurant runs out of a gas station.*

Bottom left: *Years on the barbeque competition circuit helped the Stehney's master their recipes.*

Bottom center: *Owners Jeff and Joy Stehney.*

Bottom right: *Their ribs have won all sorts of national awards. All images courtesy Joe's Kansas City*

onion rings, and smoked meat inside a bun. Kansas City Chiefs quarterback Patrick Mahomes rates it as one of his favorite meals and says he orders it once every two weeks.

The Stehney's have expanded their growing barbecue empire to locations in Olathe and Leawood, and they also cater nationwide. In a town filled with dozens of great-tasting barbecue joints, Joe's Kansas City has found a way to stand above them all.

3002 W 47th Ave., Kansas City, KS, 913-722-3366
joeskc.com

The Z Man is named after radio host Mike Zarrick. Jeff Stehney created the unique sandwich and asked Z-Man, as he was called, to hold a contest on-air to name it. All the entries were terrible. Customers came in asking for the Z-Man sandwich, and that's the name that stuck.

FLUFFY FRESH DONUTS

Making donuts the old-fashioned way

His dad's original neon sign hangs in the front window of his small donut shop in Mission. It glows red and reads, "Fluffy Fresh Donuts," a daily reminder of the man who taught him how to bake.

Jim Hollinger opened the most popular donut shop in Kansas City back in 1990. Before that, he sold Coors beer, but he tired of it and wanted to return to his roots. He had fond memories of his dad's donut shop, where they spent many hours during his childhood making donuts together in the early morning hours. But Jim's dad retired before Jim could come of age and take over, so his dad sold the shop to an employee. Years later, Jim decided to open his own donut shop in Mission, Kansas, using his father's original recipes.

Jim's father, Joe, learned the donut trade while working at "Dixie Cream" donuts during the Great Depression. That's where he courted Jim's mom, who also worked there. They eventually saved enough money to buy the donut shop, changed the name to "Fluffy Fresh," and bought the red neon sign as a way to lure customers inside, where they could smell the fresh dough baking in the back.

Like his father, Jim only uses the best, most expensive ingredients for his donuts, like hard wheat flour and fudge-based frosting. He doesn't use machines; he kneads the dough, rolls it, and cuts it all by hand every day starting at midnight. On most days, all the donuts are sold out by 9:30am.

Numerous publications mention "Fluffy Fresh" as serving the best donuts in the metro. Some have called his glazed donuts the best in the world. If you want to try them, get there early. And get there fast. Jim is now in his 70s with no succession plan in place for when he retires. He has no kids to take over the family business.

Top left: *The glazed donut recipe originated during the Great Depression.*

Bottom left: *The donuts sell fast every morning so if you're not one of the first in line, you might miss out.*

Top center: *The store is in a strip mall off Johnson Drive in Mission.*

Top right: *Jim makes all the donuts by hand rather than using a machine.*

Bottom right: *Owner Jim Hollinger.*

The wear and tear of making donuts caused him to have rotator cuff surgery, but he keeps making them. Donuts are his passion, and he plans to continue sharing his delectable donuts with the world as long as he can.

5729 Johnson Dr., Mission, KS, 913-831-1609

There is another "Fluffy Fresh Donuts" on State Line Road in Kansas City, but they are not affiliated. A former employee of Jim's dad owns it and uses a different recipe and method to make donuts, so they don't taste the same.

GAROZZO'S

A busboy's rise to Italian restaurant king

The first things you notice when walking into Garozzo's are the pictures on the wall. There's Michael Garozzo with a big smile on his face standing next to Tony Bennett. Other pictures show Michael with Kid Rock, Bo Jackson, and Patrick Mahomes. It's a Who's Who of the rich and famous who've visited his restaurant. In the dining room, there are black and white pictures of Michael's family, generations of Garozzo's who came to America from Sicily in the early 1900s.

Michael grew up in The Hill, the Little Italy of St. Louis. His dad and uncle worked as waiters at one of the best Italian restaurants in St. Louis, Parente's Italian Village. Michael started as a busboy and idolized the owner, Lou, who always dressed to the nines. He flashed his money, had beautiful ladies draped around his arms, and hung out with local athletes. Michael wanted to be just like Lou.

In 1979, Michael's cousin opened an Italian restaurant in Kansas City and asked him to help. Michael moved here and while his cousin's restaurant didn't make it, Michael stayed in Kansas City. He met the love of his life, Maggie, and they married and had four daughters. Wanting to provide for his new family, Michael opened his namesake restaurant in 1989 in Columbus Park "on a wing and a prayer." Taking great pride in his Italian heritage, Michael painted the fire hydrants outside his restaurant red, white, and green. The city took issue with it, and the *Kansas City Star* wrote up an article. Michael's picture landed

> For more than 20 years, *Ingram's* has awarded Garozzo's the Gold Medal for Best Italian Food in Kansas City. Trip Advisor and *KC Mag* also rank Garozzo's the best Italian restaurant in KC while Zagat ranks them as one of the best in the country.

Top left: *Owner Michael Garozzo with his wife and four daughters.*

Bottom left: *Michael created chicken spiedini, his signature dish, to meet the demand for healthier food.*

Top right: *Many of the pasta dishes are made fresh from traditional Sicilian recipes.*

Bottom right: *Pictures of Michael's family and ancestors cover the walls. All images courtesy Garozzo's*

on the front page, and he became an instant celebrity. After that, business boomed. Michael welcomed a full house every night.

His signature dish is the chicken spiedini. When Michael first created his menu, he only offered a beef and veal spiedini, but the trend in food was toward healthier eating and white meat. His uncle suggested he cook up chicken spiedini even though no other Italian restaurant did it. It tasted so good that it became his most requested dish. Most of his recipes come from family. The others are the best dishes from the other Italian restaurants he's worked at over the years. Customers can now enjoy an authentic Italian meal while listening to the Rat Pack and watching Michael work the room, making sure everyone feels like family.

526 Harrison St., Kansas City, MO, 816-221-2455
garozzos.com

ARTHUR BRYANT'S

"The single best restaurant in the world."

Kansas City is considered the barbecue capital of the world thanks to Arthur Bryant.

Arthur didn't invent barbecue. His boss did. Henry Perry learned how to smoke meat as a young child in the south. It was popular there but not here. When Henry landed in Kansas City in the early 1900s, he served barbecue to workers who'd never eaten it before. He later opened a restaurant called "Perry's Barbeque" and hired Charlie Bryant as a chef. Charlie recruited his brother, Arthur, to join him. When Perry died in 1940, Charlie took over the business. Six years later, he sold it to Arthur.

The first thing Arthur did was sweeten the BBQ sauce. Perry's vinegar-based sauce was too hot and peppery for many. Adding molasses made the sauce sweeter. Then in 1968, Arthur moved into an old bakery at 17th and Brooklyn and renamed the restaurant Arthur Bryant's. He offered large portions of smoked meat and made all the sandwiches in front of the customers. He gave away the burnt end shavings from the meats. That's how burnt ends came to be. In 1972, journalist Calvin Trillin for the *New Yorker* called Arthur Bryant's "the single best restaurant in the world" and said the best meat was the burned ends of the brisket you could eat for free. (They no longer give it out for free like Arthur used to do.)

Arthur Bryant's was also the first integrated restaurant in Kansas City at a time when segregation reigned. His restaurant sat

> Arthur used to mix his sauce in the restaurant and then store it in five-gallon glass jars. Big glass jars of his sauce sit in the restaurant's windows today, its only decoration.

Top left: *The restaurant has been in an old bakery building since 1968.*

Bottom left: *Bryant used to give the burnt ends away for free.*

Center: *A cook offers a customer the Beef and Fry.*

Top right: *The Beef and Fry is their best seller.*

Bottom right: *Founder Arthur Bryant. Courtesy Arthur Bryant's Restaurant*

near Municipal Stadium, and all the ballplayers and fans—Black and white—ate there after games. Countless Hollywood celebrities and presidents have tasted Arthur's meats. Arthur never married nor had children. He invested his life into his restaurant and oversaw the cooking of 2,000 pounds of meat daily. If he took a vacation, he shut the restaurant down until he returned. He literally gave his heart to his passion. In 1982, he died inside his restaurant from a heart attack.

The tradition of Arthur's "grease house" continues today. Their best seller is the Beef and Fry, slow-cooked brisket with hand-cut fries fried in lard. The spareribs rubbed with sugar and brown sugar are also popular. The current owners want to stay true to this iconic eatery by offering a simple meal that is plentiful, good, and priced to sell.

1727 Brooklyn Ave., Kansas City, MO, 816-231-1123
arthurbryantsbbq.com

GRINDERS BY STRETCH

Blending art with good taste

Grinders is a fusion of art and food, and it's the creation of an artist who loves both.

STRETCH (yes, he spells his name with all capital letters) didn't want to grow up to be a starving artist, so he learned to cook at a young age. As a teenager in Philadelphia, he manned the grill at the Woolworths lunch counter, frying up Philly cheesesteaks and grinders. What's a grinder, you ask? It's a hot sub sandwich with bread so thick, you have to grind your teeth through it to eat it. After high school, STRETCH enrolled in the Kansas City Art Institute. He moved here and learned to sculpt. As a starving college student with bills to pay, he blended his creativity with his love of food and entranced his classmates by grilling sandwiches with flat irons and cooking hot dogs on hot nails. He then went to Virginia Commonwealth University to get his Master of Fine Arts degree, and while there he built sculptures by day and cooked/bartended by night.

After graduation, STRETCH moved back to Kansas City and opened a sculpting studio in the Crossroads District, a place where many up-and-coming artists went to create. But there was no restaurant nearby serving inexpensive food where an artist could hang out. So in 2004, STRETCH opened Grinders. It's an eclectic blend of art, food, and music with a dive bar-type atmosphere.

> Besides food, STRETCH also is well-known in the art world for his large-scale sculptures. You can see his artwork outside the H&R Block Headquarters, the Woodsweather Bridge, Heritage Trail, and the Unified Government of Wyandotte County.

Top left: *Chef Guy Fieri parked outside Grinders in the Crossroads.*

Bottom left: *STRETCH likes to experiment with different toppings on his New York-style pizza.*

Top center: *The smashed burgers are very popular.*

Bottom center: *A grinder.*

Right: *Owner STRETCH. All images courtesy Grinders by STRETCH*

His signature menu item is, of course, the Grinder. The bread is shipped in from Philadelphia to re-create the cheesesteaks of his youth. The menu is very eclectic, with New York-style pizza, award-winning barbecue, "death wings," and smashed burgers. Everything is cooked fresh and off the grill in minutes. STRETCH has a line of hot sauces that have been featured on the Food Network and *Diners, Drive-Ins and Dives*, and he's toured with Guy Fieri twice. He's also traveled the world to get fresh ideas, eating goat with the Masai tribe in Africa and shaving pigs in the Republic of Georgia.

By fusing art, music, and food, STRETCH has created a safe place for people from all walks of life to come together and try different types of food in a fun, artistic environment.

417 E 18th St., Kansas City, MO, 816-472-5454
grinderspizza.com

HARVEY'S/PIERPONT'S

Two restaurants forged by history

Union Station is arguably the most beautiful building in Kansas City. Built in 1914, it was one of the busiest train stations in the country with more than 270 trains passing through each day. In the 1970s, that number fell to six trains a day, and Union Station fell into disrepair. Some thought it might be best to tear it down. But in 1999, the city voted to save it, and as part of the renovations, they opened two restaurants—Harvey's and Pierpont's.

Harvey's sits where the railway-ticket booking counter used to be. The open-air, two-story restaurant gives customers an amazing view of the beautiful architecture of this iconic building. It was originally called Union Café, but the Brancato family took over in 2009 and re-created the look and feel of an old train-stop restaurant. They named it Harvey's in honor of Fred Harvey, who in the late 1800s owned 80 restaurants along rail stops across the country. Unlike other diners near the tracks, his places were clean and served good food on white linen and fine china. The waitresses wore black and white uniforms and were called Harvey girls. Mr. Harvey gave young women an opportunity to move west and make a decent living doing honest work. While the waitresses at Harvey's today don't wear the same uniforms, they still serve great food.

Harvey's only serves breakfast and lunch. For dinner, you can go to nearby Pierpont's. Named after the great Wall Street tycoon J.P. Morgan (his middle name was Pierpont), this restaurant is located in the former women's "retiring room"—a place for women to relax while avoiding the stares of men. In the 1970s, as train travel became less popular, a restauranteur turned the space into an upscale eatery called the Lobster Pot. His son later took over and changed the name to Colony Steakhouse, and they used the lady's bathtubs from the retiring room to hold the salad bar.

Top left: *Union Station in the 1940s. The ticket booth (right) is where Harvey's currently sits.*
Courtesy Union Station

Bottom left: *Fried chicken is a popular menu item at Harvey's. Courtesy Harvey's*

Top right: *Cinnamon pancakes. Courtesy Harvey's*

Bottom right: *Pierpont's was originally a woman's retiring room for weary train travelers.*
Courtesy Pierpont's

But in 1989, the restaurant shut down. When they renovated Union Station, the city asked the Hereford House to open a restaurant inside. They named it Pierpont's and brought in turn-of-the-century décor, including a 30-foot-tall mahogany bar, a private wine cellar, a booth room, and a lounge. And if you pick the right night, you can dine with live jazz playing in the background. For all these reasons, Harvey's and Pierpont's have become culinary jewels in this elegant, historic spot.

30 W Pershing Rd., Kansas City, MO, 816-460-2274
harveyskc.com/Pierponts.com

> When you are seated at Harvey's, they give you crayons so you can draw on the white paper tablecloth as you wait for your food.

THE SAVOY AT 21C

The newest oldest restaurant in town

Arising from the ashes, Kansas City's oldest restaurant refuses to die.

The Savoy Grill opened back in 1903. John and Charles Arbuckle, the owners of the Arbuckle Coffee Company, had built the Savoy Hotel 14 year earlier, and due to high demand they decided to build a restaurant right next door. The Savoy Grill quickly earned a reputation as Kansas City's premier seafood and steak place. It had a carved-oak bar and high-beamed ceiling, and celebrities like W.C. Fields, Will Rogers, and Paul Newman all ate here whenever they visited Kansas City. The stunning architecture, warm atmosphere, and aged steaks attracted a Who's-Who list of customers. The Savoy Grill also became a favorite of a young Harry Truman, who applied to work as a waiter but didn't get the job. He would later eat lunch here during his break from the nearby haberdashery he owned, where he measured and sold suits. After he became President, he continued visiting the Savoy Grill with his wife Bess whenever they returned home. Over the years, the hotel and restaurant changed owners, but they all embraced the history of this beautiful building.

But then in 2014, tragedy struck.

A kitchen fire destroyed part of the building. Some feared the Savoy Grill would never reopen. But 21c Museum Hotels out of Louisville, Kentucky, which now owned the building, spent the

---

When making reservations, request the "No. 4 President's Booth." It was Harry Truman's favorite spot, and Warren G. Harding, Gerald Ford, and Ronald Reagan also ate in this booth.

Left: *The menu constantly changes based on what's in season.*

Top center: *A postcard showing the original Savoy hotel.*

Top right: *A Sunday brunch of pork and sweet potato hash with two sunnies.*

Bottom right: *The restaurant reopened after a fire in 2014 severely damaged the building.*
All images courtesy 21c Museum Hotels

next four years renovating it. They took great care to preserve its history. In 2018, it reopened as part of a new concept: a hotel–museum–restaurant. Visitors can now book a room, peruse local contemporary art in a connected museum space, and then walk down the hallway to eat a meal at the restored Savoy.

Despite smoke damage from the fire, the owners were able to preserve a lot of the wood paneling, columns, stained glass windows, solid oak bar, and front-room booths. They even restored some of the 12 original murals Edward Holslag painted in 1903 that depict pioneers on the Santa Fe Trail. When you walk in today, it looks much like it did when it first opened more than 120 years ago, when it was the place to eat in KC.

219 W 9th St., Kansas City, MO, 816-443-4260
thesavoykc.com

CHRISTOPHER ELBOW CHOCOLATES

Chocolate art to admire and taste

They're too beautiful to eat. Colorful, decadent, flavorful chocolates created by a man who has turned candy-making into an art form.

Christopher Elbow didn't start as a chocolatier. When he was 12 years old, the Kansas City native dreamed of becoming a world-famous chef. He apprenticed under some of the best in the business, working in Las Vegas for Emeril Legasse and Jean Joso. He then returned to Kansas City to work as a pastry chef at the five-star American Restaurant. That's where he taught himself how to make chocolates. The customers loved them, and he discovered he'd stumbled onto something unique. But then it hit him: burnout. He was spending too many long days and nights in the kitchen. In 2003, Christopher contemplated quitting the business and going back to school to become an architect, but he decided to spend one year seeing if he could make the chocolate business work.

Christopher didn't want to make typical chocolates. He wanted to mix bright colors with fancy flavors to turn every chocolate creation into a masterpiece. To find inspiration, he visited museums to discover new shapes, colors, and textures. He added exotic flavors like fresh lemon, Vietnamese cinnamon, macadamia

> Christopher supports small cacao farmers from around the world. He's visited several suppliers to ensure they treat their workers well and don't use child labor or slaves to pick the cacao beans.

Left: *Owner Christopher Elbow*

Center: *Exotic flavors and bright colors elevate these chocolates above all others. Courtesy Christopher Elbow Chocololates*

Top right: *Christopher offers seasonal flavors in beautiful boxes.*

Bottom right: *Each piece of chocolate looks like a work of art.*

praline, lavender, Aztec spice, butterscotch bourbon, Irish coffee, banana lime rum, fig honey, pistachio cherry, and Yuzu mandarin. Is your mouth watering yet?

When Christopher first started, he made all his chocolates in a small kitchen connected to his downtown store. But due to high demand, he quickly ran out of space and moved his operations into another building with more room to cook. He installed a test kitchen near his office so he can experiment with new flavors whenever he desires.

Not satisfied with just bon-bons, Christopher is always flexing his creative muscles. He opened an artisan ice cream and donut shop in Fairway, Kansas, called Fairway Creamery, and then sold it. He's partnered with Boulevard Brewery to create a Chocolate Ale that sells during Valentine's Day. He's worked with the Roasterie to create a chocolate-infused coffee. He loves collaboration. He also loves living his dream, not as a world-famous chef but as a world-famous chocolatier.

1819 McGee St., Kansas City, MO, 816-842-1300
elbowchocolates.com

THE TOWN COMPANY

A new concept at a historic hotel

They used to socialize in this place. Celebrities. Dignitaries. Presidents Harry Truman and Dwight D. Eisenhower. Mob boss Tom Prendergast. Former Royals owner Ewing Kauffman. They all belonged to the Kansas City Social Club, which built a 14-story clubhouse at the corner of 13th and Baltimore in 1922. Members came here to play cards, smoke, drink, and talk. They could enjoy the five-lane swimming pool on the 13th floor, bowl in the basement, eat dinner on the rooftop terrace, and stay the night in one of the rooms. But by 2002, club membership had dwindled. A developer bought the building and turned it into apartments. Hyatt later took over and spent millions to preserve the beauty of the place. They restored the Tudor Ballroom with its stained glass windows, the Grill Room with its murals of medieval scenes, and the President's Room with its rich woodwork and fireplace.

The busts of famous Social Club members now decorate the gorgeous lobby, where a beautiful bar straight out of Manhattan, New York, invites you to sit for a pre-dinner drink. The ornate wooden alcove where cigars were once sold is now a coffee shop serving pastries. Where the old row of phone booths used to sit is now a restaurant called the Town Company. The name is a nod to Kansas City history. In 1838, as people moved to this part of the country, the Town of Kansas Company formed nearby. The Company owned the land and wondered what to call this new town. Rabbitville, Possum Trot, and Port Fonda were all considered, but they ended up calling it the Town of Kansas, which later became Kansas City.

Just like they did in the old days, the Town Company cooks their meals over a large, wood-fired hearth that burns local

Top left: *There used to be telephone booths where the restaurant now sits.*

Bottom left: *Chicken, sweet corn, oyster mushrooms, jalapenos, and purslane.*

Bottom center: *Duck breast and sausage with fennel, orange, turnip and sorrel.*

Top right: *Every dish, like this chile-smoked country pork chop, is filled with flavor.*

Bottom right: *The restaurant is in the back of Hotel Kansas City, a former social club for the wealthy and well-known. All images courtesy The Town Company*

Missouri white oak. The food is fantastic, and their vegetable dishes with tartare have become fan favorites, as has the smoked egg with trout roe. When you break the egg, a silky yolk flows out, and you can scoop out the decadent bites. The best part? The Town Company's rotating menu is supplied by local farmers and ranchers, keeping this restaurant truly local.

1228 Baltimore Ave., Kansas City, MO, 816-895-0381
hotelkc.com

> After dinner, head downstairs to Nighthawk. It's a fun lounge with a cool 1950s vibe. On some nights they play records out of a World War II speaker. On other nights it's live bands.

CHAPPELL'S RESTAURANT AND SPORTS MUSEUM

One of the best sports bars in America

Hundreds of football helmets representing NFL, college, and high school teams from across the country hang from the rafters at Chappell's. There are 1,001 helmets total. Why 1,001? Because when Jim Chappell first opened his sports bar, *USA Today* ranked the *top* sports bars in the country and while Chappell's was on the list, the top sports bar had 1,000 helmets hanging from the ceiling. Wanting to one-up them, Jim immediately went out and collected 1,000 helmets—plus one.

Jim started out as an insurance salesman but always dreamed of owning a sports bar. In 1986, he noticed the storefront across the street from his office for sale. On an impulse, he bought it and filled the place with sports memorabilia so it would look like it had been around for years. Local sports fans packed Chappell's right away. They loved the pictures and articles of past glories plastered on the walls. Every sports memorabilia collector in the country knew Jim, as he constantly called them for Kansas City treasures. After collecting more than 10,000 items, he added the term *sports museum* to his restaurant.

Wanting to see their stuff on his walls, many Kansas City athletes—and players from other teams—visited. Joe Montana stopped for lunch every Saturday before going to the airport for

> Jim originally opened Chappell's as a politics AND sports-themed bar and grill but quickly dropped the politics theme. He didn't have enough room for political memorabilia, too!

Top left: *Curly-Q fries go great with their bacon cheeseburger.*

Bottom left: *The London Broil has been on the menu since the beginning.*

Center: *Owner Jim Chappell with hundreds of helmets hanging from the rafters behind him.*

Top right: *Sports memorabilia covers every inch of wall space.*

Bottom right: *The steak soup was on the original menu and is still served today.*

away games. Len Dawson and George Brett visited often. Sports radio hosts did live shows inside and invited athletes to join them. If word got out a famous athlete was there, fans would wait outside to get an autograph.

While the memorabilia gets customers through the door, the food keeps them coming back. Zagat once ranked Jim's burger the best in Kansas City. The London Broil (flank steak), steak soup, and pork tenderloin have been on the menu since the beginning. And don't forget the curly-Q fries! When they tried to replace them with a different kind of fry, so many people complained they decided to leave them alone.

In 2018, Jim retired and sold his restaurant. He kept a few sentimental items but left the rest behind. The new owners add new items to the walls each year, like items from the Chiefs 2019 Super Bowl victory. Jim's dream is in good hands, as customers will enjoy these sports memories for years to come.

323 Armour Rd., North Kansas City, MO, 816-421-0002
chappellskc.com

CARDBOARD CORNER CAFÉ

Gourmet gameplay

In the game of Life, Chase and Madeline Davis are not Sorry they took a Risk to create a Monopoly.

Game lovers in college, the newlyweds dreamed of someday opening a board-game café. They saved up their money, formed a Stratego, and went to the bank to get a loan—but they had Trouble. Every bank said no. They were too young. Too inexperienced. Didn't have a Clue. Crushed, they threw the dice one last time and it came up Yahtzee—thanks to Phil and Lynn Kilgore.

The Kilgores owned a board game store in Overland Park called TableTop Game and Hobby. They'd run it successfully for more than 20 years. When a mutual friend told them about the Davis's plight, they decided to become mentors and offered to help. The storefront next door to TableTop was empty. If Chase and Madeline put their café there, they could combine forces with the Kilgores and attract gamers to both establishments. Checkmate! With a Ticket to Ride in hand, the Davises were able to fulfill their dream thanks to the Kilgores's investment.

But opening a new business in 2020 proved a real Trivial Pursuit since it happened during the pandemic. To attract Hungry, Hungry Hippos, they created an enticing menu centered around artisan waffles. Their unique creations turned the café into a real Candy Land. Flavors include Fruity Pebbles, lemon blueberry poppy seed, peaches and cream, pina colada, and root beer float. You can also get something more adventurous, like the Jalapeno Popper, Pizza, Buffalo Chicken, or Avocado Toast waffles. And the craft drinks! They come with or without alcohol and are all named after games. The Dragon's Breath is a black tea lemonade with raspberry and peach. The Tsuro of the Sea Breeze is a combination of fruit and vodka.

Top left: *Owners Chase and Madeline Davis, in back, play games with friends.*

Bottom left: *Not every waffle they offer is sweet. Others are savory, like the "wacho" with taco meat, pico, and sour cream.*

Top right: *You can build your own waffle from an assortment of fruits, sweets, and syrups.*

Bottom right: *You can play one of 700 games while eating a S'Mores waffle. All images courtesy Cardboard Corner Cafe*

The gameplay is free. You don't need a Password and it's certainly not Taboo to bring a friend. Just grab a game and a table and play to your Hearts content. Just don't forget to Speak Out if you get hungry or thirsty. The Catchphrase? Waffles.

9240 Metcalf Ave., Overland Park, KS, 913-283-7081
cardboardcornerkc.com

Their 700-game collection ranges from the classics to little-known gems like Gloomhaven and Twilight Imperium. If you want to take a game home? Go next door to TableTop Game and Hobby and buy it from the Kilgores.

IN-A-TUB

Powdered cheese takes these tacos to the next level

Before serving the best tacos in Kansas City, In-A-Tub specialized in ice cream. That's where it got its name. When it first opened in 1951, customers would walk up to the window to order. The small ice cream shop served 50 different flavors and scooped the ice cream into a molded fiber "tub." Customers would then sit outside or in their cars and eat it.

In 1957, Marian Carpenter bought the restaurant and got rid of the ice cream. She decided to instead specialize in pocket burgers, a loose meat sandwich. She added tacos to the menu as an afterthought. To her surprise, the tacos quickly became her best-selling item. Customers loved the unique taste produced when Marian dipped the tacos in a fryer and then sprinkled them with powdered cheese on top. Why powdered cheese? The store was so small, she didn't have enough room in the refrigerator to hold freshly shredded cheese. Powdered cheese is shelf-stable. It's similar to the coating on Cheetos—it's addictive, and customers loved it.

In the 1980s, the Scruby family approached Marian and asked if they could pay her to franchise In-A-Tub. She agreed. The Scruby's got aggressive and built more than two dozen In-A-Tubs across the metro area. While they were very popular, the Scruby's extended themselves too much financially, and in the 1990s, they started shutting them down. Aaron Beeman worked as a cook at one of the In-A-Tubs, and in 1996, he offered to buy a store from the Scruby family. Then in 2001, Aaron bought Marian's store. Today, these are the only two stores left. They currently sit blocks away from each other on North Oak Street.

Left: *Owner Aaron Beeman. Courtesy In-A-Tub*

Center: *In-A-Tub after Marian Carpenter turned it into a taco stand in the late 1950s. Courtesy In-A-Tub*

Top right: *The pocket burger is a loose meat sandwich with cheese and pickles.*

Bottom right: *Their tacos are fried and topped with a delicious cheese powder.*

Since buying the restaurants, Aaron hasn't changed anything about the recipes or menu. He makes the food the same way they did back in 1957. He sees himself as the curator of In-A-Tub's past, and he's installed plaques on the wall to tell the story of this small drive-thru. Many remember when this was the only place serving tacos, and whenever they get a hankering for fried tacos with powdered cheese, they know exactly where to go.

4000 N Oak St., Kansas City, MO, 816-452-2149
8174 NW Prairie View Rd., Kansas City, MO, 816-436-5888

In-A-Tub was one of the first fast-food restaurants in Kansas City. While they still sell pocketburgers, ice cream, and other items, tacos make up the majority of their sales.

DIXON'S FAMOUS CHILI

The most famous chili in town

Want ketchup on your chili?

If you put the red stuff on your meal at Dixon's Famous Chili, you'll be fined 15 cents. That's a small price to pay considering how it used to be. For decades, Dixon's founder, Vergne Dixon, banned all ketchup from his restaurant. Why? He didn't want customers ruining his unique chili flavor. And if he caught them sneaking it in, he'd kick them out.

Vergne first started selling his great-tasting chili out of a street cart in downtown Kansas City during the turn of the century. In 1919, he opened his first restaurant called "Dixon's Chili Parlor" on 15th and Olive. Vergne perfected his chili recipe and focused on fast service—get them in, get them out. His chili business thrived. While he mostly served the working man, celebrities soon took note and stopped by. President Harry Truman became his most famous customer when, in 1952, *Life Magazine* took pictures of Truman enjoying the chili at Dixon's. The writer called it "Dixon's Famous Chili" in the article, and the name stuck.

Vergne kept the business in the family and recruited his relatives to help run it. In 1961, his nephew, Leonard Totta, took over and opened a second restaurant in Independence. (That's the only store still open today.) Pressured by customers to let them

> **Whenever President Truman visited, he would order the tamale spread, their most popular dish. You can eat it either "dry" or "wet." Just ask the waitress the difference and she'll explain.**

Top left: *A mural on the side of the restaurant thanks customers for more than 100 years of service.*

Bottom left: *You can get your chili dry or wet. You can also add sauces and condiments to make it taste even better.*

Top right: *Some say their taco sauce is the best in the business.*

Bottom right: *The original Dixon's Chili at 15th and Olive with founder Vergne Dixon standing outside. Courtesy Dixon's Famous Chili.*

use ketchup, Totta relented—as long as they paid the 15-cent fine, which is still instituted. Besides chili, Dixon's also serves all-you-can-eat tacos made from the same meat but seasoned a little spicier with a sauce they call "the G.O.A.T of all taco sauces." You be the judge.

Five generations of Vergne's family have worked here, and it is currently the longest-running family-owned business in Kansas City. Vergne's descendants take pride in serving great-tasting chili, and they have no plans to slow down any time soon.

9105 E Hwy. 40, Independence, MO, 816-861-7308
dixonschili.com

THE GOLDEN SCOOP

A "special" need for ice cream

They call themselves Super Scoopers, and they greet every customer with a smile and a wave. There's a beauty in each of their friendly faces. Every employee at The Golden Scoop has a developmental disability. But despite their personal challenges, they make a living doing something they love: helping others.

The concept of a nonprofit ice cream/coffee shop staffed solely by people with special needs came from the mind of Lindsay Krumholz. A special education teacher by trade, Lindsay saw many of her students struggling to find gainful employment after graduation. The unemployment rate among this group of people is around 80 percent, and many of the jobs available are menial, assembly-line type work.

Lindsay had heard of a coffee shop on the East Coast and a creamery in Texas that hired people with developmental disabilities. She decided to marry the two concepts. She recruited her sister, Amber Schreiber, to create a nonprofit so they could re-invest all their profits back into their employees. They've hired more than 20 people with special needs, and there is a waiting list of others who want to join the Super Scooper team. Many even come in on their days off to spend more time with their fellow co-workers and customers.

As for the coffee and ice cream, the Super Scoopers make it fresh daily—and it tastes great! They serve unique flavors like Dunkel Ice Cream, a collaboration with KC Bier; Rum Cake Ice Cream, a collaboration with Jude's Rum Cakes; and Lucy 41, their only dairy-free option. It's named after Lucy, an employee who is lactose intolerant. The 41 stands for how many tries it took to create the perfect taste.

Top left: *They only hire people with special needs to sell muffins, coffee, and ice cream. Courtesy The Golden Scoop*

Bottom left: *Managers oversee the Super Scoopers as they make a drink for a customer.*

Top right: *The Super Scoopers make the ice cream fresh daily.*

Bottom right: *Lucy has her own ice cream flavor called Lucy 41, for those who are lactose intolerant.*

Lindsay hopes to open more Golden Scoops around Kansas City and create even more job opportunities for those facing unique challenges. And she hopes to keep changing the lives of those with special needs and her customers one scoop at a time.

9540 Nall Ave., Overland Park, KS, 913-283-8044
thegoldenscoop.org

The Golden Scoop owners recruit volunteers to mentor the employees. They are not paid but volunteer their time to guide and teach the workers with special needs how to best do their jobs.

PONAK'S

Serving World-Class Margaritas since 1975

John Ponak got into the Mexican food business by accident. When he first opened his namesake bar and restaurant in 1975, John hired a cook from Town Topic to grill burgers. When that cook left a year later, he put out an ad for a short-order cook. A Mexican family answered it and suggested he serve traditional Mexican food instead. John sampled the recipes, loved them, and hired them to create a new menu.

At that time, his Mexican restaurant was one of the only ones in Kansas City, and it sat in the perfect location. For decades, Mexican immigrants who moved to Kansas City to work for the railroad settled their families near Southwest Boulevard. Many of them now went to Ponak's to eat. John's success created a new demand for Mexican food, and many other Mexican restaurants soon opened nearby.

John was born and raised in Kansas City. His parents owned a bar for most of his young life, and he grew up helping them run it. At the age of 15, he briefly worked as a busboy for Los Corrals, Kansas City's oldest Mexican Restaurant. It was there that he cultivated his love for Mexican food. After high school, John enlisted in the Marines and fought in Vietnam. While overseas, he dreamed of someday owning a restaurant. When his tour of duty ended in 1970, he moved back home and five years later bought a small bar on Southwest Boulevard. At first he only owned half the building, but when demand for his tasty Mexican cuisine grew, he bought the rest of it and built a colorful dining room to seat more people. When you visit, you'll notice the parking lot is small and the entrance is in the back. It's a bit of an odd setup. But once you step inside, you'll meet a friendly staff whose only goal is to make

Left: *Owner John Ponak.*

Top center: *While the front of the restaurant is inviting, the entrance is actually in the back.*

Bottom center: *John originally served burgers but quickly transitioned to enchiladas after hiring a Mexican chef.*

Top right: *Sit outside and sip on a "World Class" margarita.*

Bottom right: *You can get all kinds of traditional Mexican dishes smothered in cheese. All images courtesy Ponak's*

sure you have a good time. It can get loud as everyone talks and laughs while enjoying great food and drinks.

Speaking of drinks, John's special margarita mix has won numerous awards. He trademarked it as "World-Class" and sells between 10,000-and-20,000 gallons of it every year. His tacos and tamales have also won awards, as has his restaurant. Ponak's might be one of the oldest Mexican restaurants in Kansas City, but it shows no signs of slowing down.

2856 Southwest Blvd., Kansas City, MO, 816-753-0775
ponaksmexicankitchen.com

> **Ponak's bought the first-ever keg made by Boulevard Beer. The restaurant sits a couple blocks from where John McDonald brewed his first batch of Pale Ale. Today, Ponak's always has Boulevard and other local beers on tap.**

BISTRO 303/THE PEACOCK

Cooking up gay pride for all to see

At the age of 63, Gene Switzer had had enough. As a gay man living in Kansas City, he was tired of ducking into dark, seedy bars for dinner and a cocktail with others in the LGBT community. He didn't want to hide any longer. He wanted a bright, clean place where he could dine with confidence. He teamed up with his friend, Jeffrey Schmitz, to open the city's first gay bar and restaurant with clear glass windows in front. He wanted everyone walking by to look in and see the great food they were eating. He wanted everyone to see how much fun they were having. Instead of being a well-kept secret within the gay community, he wanted their restaurant to be known to everyone.

Gene and Jeffrey opened Bistro 303 in 2003, and the city embraced them right away. Both gay and straight patrons visited their French bistro for a fancy cocktail and a great meal cooked by Chef Paul Mullins. Paul had run the kitchen at the restaurant (called Metropolis City Grill) that had previously occupied the space where Bistro 303 is located. Gene and Jeffrey asked him to stay and run the kitchen for their new concept, and he agreed. They gave him the freedom to create a fun menu mixing traditional bar food with French cuisine. You can get a burger with chicken wings or a roast beef French dip with pommes frites.

Encouraged by their success, Gene and Jeffrey decided to expand. They bought the space next door, and in 2021, they turned it into The Peacock. Instead of copying the loud, social atmosphere at Bistro 303, they decided to offer a quiet, intimate experience in cozy quarters. The room is small—they can only serve 48 people at one time. At The Peacock, they serve comfort food with an international twist, using all types of herbs and spices to give

Left: *Bistro 303 offers a diverse menu. Courtesy Bistro 303*

Top center: *The food at the Peacock has a Mideastern flair, such as the za'atar seasoned pork, squash puree, and fried brussels sprouts with agave cider butter.*

Bottom center: *The owners intentionally installed glass windows so the gay community would no longer have to hide when going out.*

Right: *Owners Gene Switzer and Jeffrey Schmitz. Courtesy Bistro 303*

old favorites a new taste. Dishes like lamb shank, pork chops, and salmon are cooked in the Thai, African, and Mediterranean traditions, and The Peacock offers unique appetizers like beet hummus, pork belly, and fried Brussel sprouts.

Gene and Jeffrey have changed the gay culinary community with their courage to display their lifestyle for all to see. They invite everyone in the community to join them in celebrating gay pride as they continue to break down barriers—one dish at a time.

303 Westport Rd., Kansas City, MO, 816-753-2303
bistro303.com

> **The dining room at Bistro 303 showcases 22 original paintings by local artists. It took them more than 50 years to collect all these pieces, and many of them are irreplaceable.**

ITALIAN GARDENS PIZZA

Fourth time's the charm for this iconic restaurant

They called it "Kansas City's Favorite Restaurant."

For more than 80 years, Italian Gardens served great Italian food at 11th and Baltimore in downtown Kansas City. Teresa Bondon opened the restaurant in 1925. Her Sicilian recipes won over all of Kansas City, and the people came in droves. Celebrities like Frank Sinatra, Harry Truman, Billy Joel, Yogi Berra, and even Andre the Giant visited this iconic Italian eatery. Many had their pictures up on the wall, and many were a part of the Sabenadica Club. It derived from the restaurant's large Sabenadica Table, where lone travelers could grab a chair and eat together. The club grew to over 2,000 members and consisted of regulars as well as celebrities.

Through the decades, ownership passed down from Teresa to her son Ralph to her grandson John. In 2003, with the restaurant struggling to regain its past success, John Bondon decided to shut it down for good. But a few years later, the son of a long-time employee revived the Italian Gardens name using the same great recipes—albeit in different locations.

John DiCapo grew up at Italian Gardens. His dad, Carl, started working there as a cashier in 1953. Over the course of five

> Don't expect round pizza at Italian Gardens Pizza. They make it in a square. Why? It's symbolic of John's refusal to cut corners when it comes to quality. While the recipe is mostly his Aunt Teresa's, he made some modifications to make the crust light and airy.

Left: *The Vesuvius sandwich is a fan favorite.*
Right: *Owner John DiCapo with Carl DiCapo. All images courtesy Italian Gardens Pizza*

decades, Carl worked his way up to chairman of the board. When John Bondon closed the restaurant, John DiCapo took ownership and opened two smaller Italian Gardens Drive-Thru's in Overland Park and the Northland. Both failed to catch on. Next, he opened an Italian Gardens cookie factory on 19th Street in Kansas City. He then turned that into Italian Gardens Pizza. It's a small restaurant with a focus on takeout rather than eat-in. But he still uses his Great Aunt Teresa's recipes. Besides great-tasting pizza, they offer the traditional spaghetti and meatballs, ravioli made from scratch, and breaded pork cutlet and steak sandwiches.

Oh, and John kept the Sabenadica Table in his new place. His parents still visit and hold court with those who want to join them for a meal. Italian Gardens might be in a new place with a different look, but the food tastes just as it did when Teresa started making it nearly 100 years ago.

901 E 19th St., Kansas City, MO, 816-221-3507
igpizza.com

THE CORNER CAFÉ

Comfort food served with a slice of memorabilia

Walking into The Corner Café is like walking back in time. Black and white photos and artifacts on the walls tell the history of the place.

In 1936, former Riverside Mayor Ferd Filger built a Texaco gas station next to a small café at the corner of Gateway and Vivion Road. Originally called Jolly Jerry's, the café changed owners and names a couple times before Ferd's granddaughter, Kathi, and her husband, Ed Rule, bought it in 1983. They named it The Corner Café because, well, it sat on the corner.

Having never run a restaurant before, Ed and Kathi Rule went searching for good recipes. They went to potluck dinners at local churches and asked the ladies if they could serve their dishes. Other recipes came from relatives. If it tasted good, it went on the menu. People loved the homestyle flavor and packed the place. Wanting more space, Ed and Kathi built a new Corner Café in 1994 in the shape of a red barn and planted it on the same corner.

The Rules have collected tons of memorabilia from customers over the years. You might notice a chicken motif. They used to offer an all-you-can-eat chicken meal, and one customer who ordered it daily gifted Ed and Kathi a massive bronze chicken. Other customers started giving them chicken-themed gifts, too. There's also a motorcycle in the middle of the café. When a loyal customer passed away, Ed and Kathi bought it

In 2007, then-President George W. Bush visited The Corner Café. Since he'd already eaten breakfast at his hotel, he just ordered one biscuit. When he mentioned to the waitress how small it was, she quipped, "Then you should've ordered more food!"

Top left: *Nothing tops off a homestyle meal better than cherry pie a la mode. Courtesy The Corner Café*

Bottom left: *The red barn-shaped restaurant and country-style food reminds customers of grandma's cooking.*

Top center: *Besides traditional seats, customers can sit at a 1950s-style diner and watch the cooks make their food.*

Bottom center: *Breakfast is served at all times of the day. Courtesy The Corner Café*

Right: *The fried chicken is so popular, many customers have donated chicken knickknacks which now decorate the restaurant. Courtesy The Corner Café*

from his estate, and it now sits near the old Texaco gas pump honoring Kathi's grandpa, Ferd. They also brought in an old stone fireplace from Ferd's homestead and placed a windmill from the family farm out front. Antiques are everywhere, each one telling a different story.

Besides gazing at artifacts, customers can also watch their breads and desserts being made in an open kitchen at the front of the restaurant. Their cinnamon rolls have won awards, and customers love the biscuits and gravy. As for their other dishes, the chicken and the chili are their best sellers. For the Rules, it's always been about serving the kind of comfort food grandma used to make. Their success has allowed them to open two other Corner Cafés in Independence and Liberty, bringing the taste of grandma's cooking to many throughout the area.

4541 NW Gateway Ave., Riverside, MO, 816-741-2570
thecornercafe.com

THE SHIP

Ahoy! A historic dive bar finds riches in a new port

For nearly six decades, The Ship anchored in downtown Kansas City. The seafaring-themed dive bar opened in 1935. The owners decorated it like a ship, and all kinds of people came here to drink, from politicians to prostitutes and from lawmakers to lawbreakers. For a time, The Ship prospered. But in the early 1990s, with the building in disrepair, Kansas City officials decided to demolish it to make room for a federal courthouse and park. Before the wrecking ball smashed it to smithereens, the owner of the building, Adam Jones, grabbed all the ship décor and moved it to a warehouse in the West Bottoms. There it sat in storage, collecting dust for the next decade.

Ten years later, two of Adam's friends, Bob Asher and Josh Mobley, were in the West Bottoms poking around his warehouse when they found the wreckage of The Ship in the basement. Adam said they could have it, so they took it out of storage and spent the next few years looking at old pictures to put it back together inside one of Adam's warehouses. As their new ship came together, Bob and Josh started hosting private parties. As more people showed up, they decided to turn it into a bar. Next they built a kitchen, and then they expanded next door. The Ship is now as big as, well, a ship.

> The original Ship bar is highlighted in Robert Altman's movie *Kansas City*. Shortly after filming wrapped, they tore down the building, sinking The Ship's prospects in downtown KC.

Left: *Original owner Mike Salvato (right) and barman Tony Cropis (left).*

Top center: *The Ship has expanded to include an upscale bar area where bands play as people drink.*

Bottom center: *The Cubano sandwich was one of the first dishes offered when they re-opened in the West Bottoms.*

Top right: *Most of the food, like this shrimp gumbo, has a Creole theme.*

Bottom right: *The décor makes it feel as if you are eating on a ship. All images courtesy The Ship*

While seafood peppers the menu, they serve other types of food with a Caribbean/Creole theme. Fan favorites include the Cubano sandwich, the shrimp Po Boy, and the gumbo, which Bob says is the best in town. The drinks also have tropical themes, with rum subbing for whiskey in their Old Fashioned. However, they do offer traditional drinks, too, knowing that all types of sailors visit their establishment.

The ship inside The Ship does not have an official name, but Bob and Josh like to call it the S.S. *Semper Voluptarum*, which is Latin for "always for pleasure." With live bands blasting music on the weekends and food and drinks available throughout the day, they have resurrected an iconic Kansas City dive bar and continue to make it their own.

1221 Union Ave., Kansas City, MO, 816-471-7447
theshipkc.com

JACK STACK BARBECUE

It's all in the wood

Barbecue chefs use all types of wood to smoke their meats, but Fiorella's Jack Stack Barbecue uses only one kind. Hickory.

Meat smoked and cooked over hickory has a slightly stronger flavor, like bacon, and the meat chars a little darker. The hickory smoke is one reason why many call this restaurant "barbecue heaven." The aroma from the kitchen tickles the nostrils. The meat melts in the mouth. The sauces awaken the tongue. All of this, plus the leather seats and darkened atmosphere, transports you to a time when upscale, distinguished steakhouses were all the rage.

This restaurant started on its path toward widespread fame in 1957. Russ Fiorella's wife was in labor with their sixth child. He dropped her off at the hospital, and then, to her surprise, went over to 82nd and Hickman Mills Drive and bought an Inn. He turned it into a restaurant he called Smoke Stack Barbecue. A butcher by trade, Russ had a love for smoked meats and sold them out of his traditional storefront. He did not allow alcohol or telephones in his establishment, so lines of hungry customers typically formed outside. His oldest son, Jack, worked with him for many years. In 1974, Jack decided to branch off on his own and opened his first restaurant in Martin City to much acclaim. To separate his venture from his family's stores, he named it Fiorella's Jack Stack Barbecue.

To stand out from his competitors, Jack and his wife Delores smoked and cooked the meat using natural Ozark-hickory inside

> **Due to overwhelming demand for their food outside of Kansas City, Jack Stack bought a ballroom in Overland Park and renovated it to create a Catering Division. They continue to ship and cater meals at events all over the country.**

Top left: *A young Jack Fiorella, standing in front of his father, Russ, with his mouth open, would one day break out on his own.*

Bottom left: *All the meats are cooked with hickory wood.*

Top right: *Honey-glazed baby back ribs.*

Bottom right: *Sides include cheesy corn bake, hickory pit beans, and potato salad. All images courtesy Jack Stack Barbecue*

a traditional brick-oven barbecue pit. They also created the most extensive barbecue menu in the country. Besides traditional items like ribs, brisket, and burnt ends, they also smoke lamb ribs and salmon. Sides like hickory pit beans, cheesy corn bake, and potato salad are also smoke-infused. Since then, they've expanded to five total restaurants in the Kansas City area.

In a city where barbecue is king, Jack Stack's Pitmasters bring more than 100 years of combined experience to their jobs. They are dedicated to the time-honored traditions of cooking the finest meat over hickory wood and letting it bask in smoke to bring out all its natural flavors.

13441 Holmes Rd., Kansas City, MO, 816-942-9141
jackstackbbq.com

BOULEVARD BREWING TOURS & RECREATION CENTER

Join the party at KC's original craft brew

Space Camper. Berry Noir. Steep Drop. Tank 7. These are the names of some of the popular beers created by Boulevard Brewery. Founder John McDonald started brewing in 1989 out of an abandoned brick warehouse on Southwest Boulevard. That's where the brewery's name comes from. Inspired by the beers he tasted while visiting Belgium, John learned the recipes and brought them here. His first concoction—Pale Ale— exploded in popularity. Encouraged, John made more Belgian-style beers in all kinds of flavors. He expanded his brewery and added more tanks to accommodate the increased demand. He also built a tasting room where visitors touring the plant could stop by to try new flavors. But then a frustrating truth came to light.

The visitors wouldn't leave—they were having too much fun.

So, in 2016, Boulevard bought the old Skelly Oil Company building next door and transformed it into the Tours & Recreation Center. On the bottom floor of this magnificent brick building sits a gift shop and exhibit area detailing the history of the Boulevard brand in Kansas City. On the second floor is the Beer Hall, where you can try 30 different brews on tap along with new concoctions not sold in stores. And on the top floor is the Rec Deck, where you can play a game of shuffleboard or foosball with friends. And don't forget to visit the outdoor patio to soak in Kansas City's beautiful skyline.

Left: *Founder John McDonald*

Center: *Drink an established ale or try a new flavor from their test kitchen.*

Right: *Beer is an ingredient in many dishes. For instance, there is Pale Ale in the pretzel dough. All images ourtesy Boulevard*

As for the food, this is not your typical bar grub. Their chefs use fresh, local ingredients to make pretzel dogs, sliders, and brewer's boards filled with a variety of local meats and cheeses. Many of the recipes use Boulevard beers as an essential ingredient; Tank 7 is mixed in with the meat in the angus burger; Pale Ale is in the pretzel dough; Whiskey Barrel Stout is used in the barbecue pork sausage.

By the way, don't expect to watch the Royals or Chiefs game during your visit. There are no televisions here. Boulevard wants you to put down your phone and engage in conversation while drinking their beers and eating their beer-infused grub.

2534 Madison St., Kansas City, MO, 816-701-7247
boulevard.com

> Boulevard also serves a spiked seltzer called Quirk that comes in flavors like: strawberry, lemon, and basil; pear yuzu; and blackberry sage. And they sell canned cocktails called Fling (mai tai, margarita, and vodka soda, to name a few).

LE FOU FROG

The most adventurous French restaurant in KC

You'd expect frog legs at a French restaurant. Even snails. But ostrich? Stingray? Lion?

Chef Mano Rafael has an adventurous spirit . . . and ADHD, according to his wife, Barbara.

They met in New York City. Mano and his brother owned a French bistro in the West Village, and Barbara was an aspiring actress who worked there as a waitress. She fell in love with both Mano and French cuisine, and they dreamed of opening their own restaurant someday. A visit to Barbara's hometown of Kansas City in 1995 planted a seed. When their rent in New York tripled, the couple decided to move to the Midwest. And when Kansas City restaurants declined to hire Mano because they didn't think customers would like his French cooking, they decided to open their own place.

But where to set up shop? Mano loved the City Market area downtown even though tumbleweeds literally blew across the street. A realtor found them the perfect space, but to seal the deal, they also had to buy $200,000 worth of liquor stored in the building. The previous owner sold packaged alcohol and didn't want to take it with him. What to do with all those spirits? Cook with them, of course!

They opened Le Fou Frog in 1996 and quickly proved the other restaurant owners wrong. Kansas Citians *did* love French cooking. The community's support encouraged Mano to become creative with his menu and try new things. Besides offering a menu built around traditional French fare like Steak au Poivre (a Kansas City strip with peppercorn sauce), Filet le Fou (lobster meat in cheese sauce), and rack of lamb, he also creates new dishes almost nightly. The wait staff gets to try each new dish so they can tell customers (and Mano) whether it's good or not.

Top left: *Mano likes to try new recipes and can get very adventurous, sometimes serving dishes like lion, ostrich, and stingray.*

Center left: *Owners Mano and Barbara Rafael.*

Bottom left: *Every dish comes with a French flair.*

Top right: *Be their guest and sit outside in an elegant patio when the weather is nice.*

Bottom right: *Bacon wrapped scallops drenched in a soy balsamic sauce with tart pickled shallots. All images ourtesy Le Fou Frog*

By the way, the wait staff also loves to sing. It used to be that every Bastille Day (July 14, the start of the French Revolution), they would sing "Be Our Guest" to customers. Now, they sing it all the time. Just ask! They all go out of their way to prove French food is not stuffy. Just be their guest and see for yourself.

400 E 5th St., Kansas City, MO, 816-474-6060
lefoufrog.com

Le Fou means "crazy" in French, something Barbara calls Mano all the time. As for Frog, in colonial America, the Canadian French used the word for "frog" as a code word to get into their forts. The English couldn't say it properly, so that's how they caught spies.

BROWNE'S IRISH MARKETPLACE

More than luck keeps North America's oldest Irish business open

Drink a Guinness, eat a Rueben, and peruse Irish imports at America's oldest Irish business. It's not in New York or Boston. It's right here in Kansas City.

When Ed and Mary Flavin first opened their grocery store in 1887, Kansas City was a dusty small town. The couple emigrated from County Kerry, Ireland, and set up their shop in front of the family home. They offered travelers and locals fresh meat and produce. In 1901, they built a store at 33rd and Pennsylvania and called it Flavin's Market. Their daughter Margaret and her husband, James R. Browne, also from Ireland, took over the grocery in 1917. He changed the name to James R. Browne Grocery. His wife and 11 children ran the store, delivering food six days a week from 6 a.m. until 6 p.m. In the 1950s, Browne's oldest son, James R. Browne Jr., who they called Bob, took over the store.

In 1981, Bob and his wife became ill. They could no longer run the store, so their daughter Kerry took over. She was a student at UMKC at the time. Her best friend from school, John McClain, agreed to help her. Together they bought the store from her parents and made some changes. They opened a deli that serves traditional Irish fare like Reubens, Shepherd's pie, and cookies made from an old Irish family recipe. They added a small bar to pour Irish beers like Guinness, Harp, and Smithwick's. Want Irish whiskey? They have that, too. They are no longer a grocery but still sell food imported from Ireland, including popular brands like Bird's, aah Bisto, and Batchelors. They also sell clothes made in Ireland and other Irish knickknacks. Every room is filled from top to bottom with Irish

Left: *The Browne's opened their store here in 1901. Originally called Flavian's Market, it was renamed Browne Grocery in 1917.*

Top center: *Owners John McClain and Kerry Browne with their sons, Rory Browne McClain and Ian Browne McClain. Courtesy Browne's*

Bottom center: *They serve traditional Reuben sandwiches in their deli along with Irish chips and a Guinness.*

Top right: *They import most of their goods from Ireland.*

Bottom right: *Irish beers are on tap and Irish whiskeys are for sale.*

apparel, which many wear with pride whenever Browne's hosts an Irish fry—a traditional Irish breakfast. And let's not forget St. Patrick's Day, when hundreds stop in for food, spirits, and Irish swag.

Twenty years after buying the store, John and Kerry decided to marry. They now have two children they hope will one day run the store. They liken their place to Cheers because they know most of their customers by name. And they are proud to carry on the tradition of Irish hospitality that started more than 135 years ago.

3300 Pennsylvania Ave., Kansas City, MO, 816-561-0030
brownesirishmarketplace.com

> John used to deliver groceries to an elderly Irish woman who gave him soda bread as a thank you. It was so good that he asked for the recipe. She agreed on one condition—don't share the recipe. He now sells it but won't tell anyone how he makes it.

LOCAL PIG + PIGWICH

How a book convinced a five-star chef to become a butcher

One of the best tasting sandwich shops in all of Kansas City is also a butcher shop.

While working at The American, which before it closed was Kansas City's only five-star restaurant, Chef Alex Pope learned how to cut up a whole pig using a book as his guide. He soon fell in love with the lost art of butchery. When another chef told Alex he couldn't find any local businesses that made sausage, inspiration struck. Alex put his career as a chef on hold to open a butcher shop.

In 2012, he and his business partner Matt Kafka opened Local Pig in the East Bottoms. They only bought free-range animals from small local farms and took great pride in using the entire animal, nose to tail. They butchered all kinds of animals, including pigs, cows, ducks, lambs, and chickens, and they sold the cutlets to local restaurants.

Many people, though, thought Local Pig was a deli. Dozens of people stopped by every day wanting sandwiches. Tired of turning so many people away, Alex and Matt decided to give the people what they wanted. They bought a shipping container, transformed it into a stationary food truck, and called it Pigwich. It went over so well that in 2018, they moved to the City Market inside the former Winslow's barbecue joint. Their new space had enough room for both a butcher shop and an eatery. After giving

---

Kansas City Chiefs head coach Andy Reid visited Pigwich when *Diners, Drive-ins & Dives* came to town. It was the first time the producers ever allowed a guest appearance on their show.

Top left: *Alex surprises customers with an off-menu special sandwich every day.*

Top center: *Owner Alex Pope with Chiefs coach Andy Reid and Guy Fieri.*

Bottom left: *Local Pig offers many cuts of meat, using the entire animal bought from local farms.*

Top right: *Besides burgers, you can also order a unique chicken sandwich.*

Bottom right: *Pigwich is one of many small restaurants in the City Market. All images courtesy Local Pig + Pigwich*

the old building a massive deep clean (it wasn't easy wiping off five decades of barbecue grease from the walls), they opened Local Pig + Pigwich to rave reviews.

When you visit, you can watch Alex and his employees cut the meat right in front of you. Alex is also proud of his charcuterie. He takes thin slices of meat and salts them, dries them, and soaks them in vinegar to create a great taste. His top sandwiches include the Pigwich, which pays tribute to Kansas City barbecue with cilantro and chipotle aioli; the Vietnamese hoagie with pickled veggies and coconut caramel sauce; and the Big Pig, a combination of fried chicken and pulled pork topped with jalapeno slices, ranch, and barbecue sauce. It's a meat nirvana where you can eat a tasty sandwich for lunch and take home freshly cut meat for dinner.

20 E 5th St., Kansas City, MO, 816-200-1639
localpig.com

BAMBOO PENNY'S

The "steakhouse" of Thai restaurants

The life of Penny Mufuka is truly a rags-to-riches story.
Born the daughter of poor rice farmers in rural Phichit,
Thailand, Penny faced a tough choice after her father died of
cancer. She could work at a nail salon in Thailand or start a new
life in America. She'd always dreamed of chasing opportunity in
a foreign land, so with just $800 in her pocket she bought a ticket
to Kansas City. She didn't speak English, but she was determined
to succeed. She secured a job as a dishwasher at a restaurant called
Thai Place in Overland Park, but she wanted to cook. Within her
first year she was promoted to preparing appetizers. Her boss/
mentor then taught her how to cook with the wok. Her first
attempt was so bad he threw it out and said, "I wouldn't serve this
to a dog." But over time, she improved greatly and became his
right-hand (wo)man.

One New Year's Eve, a friend introduced her to Doug Mufuka,
a project manager at a logistics company. They fell in love. When
Penny asked Doug to help her buy the failing Thai Place, he agreed
on one condition: that they fly to Las Vegas and get married first.
He wanted them to be legally bound to have each other's back. She
agreed, and in 2013, they opened their first restaurant. In 2020,
they opened a second restaurant in Overland Park called KC Thai.
One year later, they opened a third restaurant in Leawood called
Bamboo Penny's, an upscale eatery she refers to as her steakhouse.

Bamboo Penny's playful menu includes Crab Rangoon filled
with chocolate cream, fried rice in half a pineapple shell, and
papaya salad. She infuses tropical flavors like pineapple, mango,
and banana into her Polynesian-inspired dishes. Her drink menu
includes creative concoctions like the blood-orange martini, the

Top left: *The pineapple rice is served inside half a pineapple.*

Bottom left: *The mango cheesecake is one of many sweet offerings for dessert.*

Center: *Owner Penny Mufuka. Courtesy Bamboo Penny's*

Top right: *You can order a fun tropical cocktail with your meal.*

Bottom right: *Penny offers a fun twist on crab Rangoon with a chocolate cream center.*

spicy pineapple mule, or the Bamboo, a combination of sherry, vermouth, and bitters.

While the main room in the restaurant features an upscale chic design, the true highlight is upstairs in the Bamboo Lounge. The bar has a retractable roof and is set against a vintage Hollywood-inspired backdrop. It allows customers to socialize with friends while sipping from a fun tropical cocktail. Thai food can be more than just takeout. At Bamboo Penny's, it can be an elegant, fun, and memorable culinary experience.

5270 W 116th Pl., Leawood, KS, 913-232-7695
bamboopennys.com

Doug quit his job to help Penny run their three restaurants. He does the financials while she runs the kitchen, and they both love to meet the customers in the front of the house.

AIXOIS BISTRO

Bringing the best of France to Kansas City

To be the best, you must learn from the best.

That has always been Emmanuel Langalde's philosophy. After graduating from a well-known culinary school in Marseilles, the ambitious French native decided he would only apply for jobs at five-star restaurants and hotels. He wanted to learn a mix of cooking techniques from the masters, so he moved from job to job. After 10 years as an apprentice, Emmanuel felt ready to go out on his own. He opened his own restaurant in Marseilles, and it flourished. For five years he nurtured it, and it became very successful. But then he decided to visit his brother in Texas—and he never went back. Why not?

He fell in love.

Emmanuel met his future wife in Austin and decided to stay in the States. She was a Kansas City native, and they moved to her hometown. He worked at Le Fou Frog while they saved up the money needed to open his own restaurant. In 2001, with enough cash in hand, Emmanuel rented out a space at the Crestwood Shops near Brookside and opened his own French bistro. He leaned on his first-class culinary training to create light dishes with fresh ingredients, making every bite an explosion of flavor. The people loved it right away. They flocked to his restaurant. In fact, on many days, he saw the same people eating there for breakfast, lunch, and dinner.

> The name of the restaurant is pronounced "Ax-wha." It literally means "man from Aix-en-Provence," which is the part of southern France where Emmanuel was born and raised.

Left: *Owner Emmanuel Langalde*

Right: *The French pastries are made fresh daily. Courtesy AIXOIS Bistro*

Besides great food, Emmanuel also credits his beautiful patio for his success. When he first opened, not a lot of restaurants offered outdoor seating. But in France, people love eating outside. He tried it, and now his patio is packed all day long. While most of his menu consists of French and Mediterranean cuisine, he also includes some American fare like burgers and BLTs. But Emmanuel doesn't settle for average. He wants every dish to be delicious. With that in mind, he takes the flavor to the next level with olive oil, fresh tomatoes, and herbs like sage, rosemary, and thyme. His most popular dishes include the trout amandine and the chicken paillard.

Emmanuel doesn't want you to leave feeling stuffed or bloated. He hopes his light, airy, tasty food puts you in a good mood—and keeps you coming back for more.

251 E 55th St., Kansas City, MO, 816-333-3305
aixois.com

MESSENGER COFFEE/ IBIS BAKERY

Watching coffee go from bean to brew

It has become *the* artisanal coffee-roasting company in Kansas City, and when you visit it's easy to see why. An open floor plan gives you the chance to witness the process of turning premium coffee beans into a cup of latte. Not only that, but you can also watch them mill grain and knead dough into delicious pastries.

Messenger Coffee is a collaboration between three small Kansas City coffee companies. Instead of competing against each other, they decided to pool their resources to create a collective and offer the best coffee in town. They work directly with small bean farms from all over the world, from Ethiopia to Thailand to El Salvador. They invest 10 percent of all their coffee bean sales back to the farmers so they can build coffee nurseries, tile fermentation tanks, and build raised beds to increase the quality of the beans they grow. They also intentionally pay above market prices so the coffee bean farmers have the financial resources to continue growing. Their investment is paying off, and the proof is in the taste. Thanks to their wide array of aromas and flavors, Messenger Coffee is quickly becoming one of Kansas City's most popular java spots.

When it first formed, the collective only sold roasted beans to cafés across the metro area. But in 2017, they bought a 100-year-

> The name *Messenger* is a nod to their relationship with coffee bean farmers. They are messengers for the farm, connecting people through coffee and helping small farmers at the same time.

Top left: *Farm Partner Julio Melendez Perez*

Bottom left: *You can get a fun foam design to top off your coffee.*

Top center: *Messenger downtown is located in a renovated auto shop.*

Bottom center: *Watch them roast the coffee beans before you drink it.*

Right: *Messenger works with small farmers in other countries and pays a little extra for their beans. All images courtesy Messenger Coffee*

old former automobile shop in the Crossroads District and turned it into a fun place for people to gather for coffee and pastries. Their sister company, Ibis Bakery, took over the first floor. Big windows up front allow customers to watch the bakers mix and shape the dough before putting it into industrial ovens. On the second floor, customers can see the massive roasters they use to bake the coffee beans. And on the rooftop deck, there are skylights and a fireplace where customers can relax and talk to friends while sipping a mocha or cappuccino.

Messenger Coffee continues to expand its footprint, opening new cafés throughout the metro area. They will also continue paying a little extra for their ingredients so the small family farmers they support can continue to prosper and provide better beans, which in turn will keep Messenger at the top of the coffee food chain.

1624 Grand St., Kansas City, MO, 913-669-9883
messengercoffee.co

KELLY'S WESTPORT INN

Get a drink in Kansas City's oldest building

A century before becoming the most popular bar in Westport, Kelly's Westport Inn served as a supply store for pioneers.

Albert Gallatin Boone opened the mercantile store in 1851 in the town of Westport, and he supplied many families heading west in covered wagons on the Santa Fe, California, and Oregon Trails. When Boone left for Colorado, other families took over the building and ran a grocery and dry goods store out of it. In 1934, it became a bar.

It was called the Westport Inn, and people would stop by at all hours of the day for a mug of beer or a shot of whiskey. In February of 1947, the owner hired Randal Kelly to be his new bartender. A native of County Clare, Ireland, Randal had a friendliness and sense of humor that won over the regulars. He became very popular, and soon they were calling the place Kelly's in his honor. By the end of the year, Randal became a partner. Even so, they didn't officially change the name to Kelly's until 30 years later. During his time behind the bar, Randal kept prices down and gave money to customers down on their luck. He called his bar a "playground for the poor man."

Randal's family grew up in this bar. His children and grandchildren all mopped floors, washed tables, and served drinks. When Randal passed away in 1988, his sons Pat and Kyle took over as owners. Today, two of Randal's grandchildren manage it. They have preserved the history of this building, which according to the Westport Historical Society is one of the oldest in Kansas City. Their only additions have been a rooftop patio and live music on Friday and Saturday nights.

Kelly's serves basic drinks. They don't even have a blender, if that tells you anything. One of their best sellers is the bloody Mary

Top left: *Guy's Snacks took over the small kitchen inside and now offer sandwiches as well as pizza into the early morning hours.*

Bottom left: *Crowds often pack into Kelly's for a cold beer.*

Top right: *Randal Kelly started behind the bar and ended up owning the place.*

Bottom right: *While Joe's Pizza is no more, you can still get a slice at Kelly's. All images courtesy Kelly's Westport Inn*

topped with Guinness. As for food, they don't have a traditional kitchen. Joe's Pizza rented out a space inside for more than 20 years, selling hungry customers greasy slices of pizza in the early morning hours. But in 2022, Guy's Deli and Pizza took over. They now sell sandwiches and pizza made with Joe's original recipe.

For decades, generations of Kansas Citians have enjoyed a night out at Kelly's, and there's no reason to think the party will ever stop.

500 Westport Rd., Kansas City, MO, 816-561-5800
kellyswestportinn.com

When you visit, ask to see George Wiedenmann. He used to own the building and visited the bar every Friday night with friends. You can find his ashes sitting inside a Ten High whiskey bottle at the bar, kept there per his request.

PIROPOS

"Compliments" to the chef

The memory of the Valentine's Day Wine Massacre is still fresh in the minds of Piropos's owners.

A beautiful couple walked into Piropos in Briarcliff Village one Valentine's Day evening for dinner and sat in the corner of the crowded restaurant. When the beautiful woman learned of her beau's unfaithfulness, she stood up and threw a glass of red wine onto his white shirt before storming off. The wine left a dark red stain on the wall behind him.

Instead of repainting the wall, owners Gary and Cristina Worden decided to leave it as a warning to all cheaters. It is now their most popular table. In fact, the victim of this heinous crime often returns to the scene with pride and explains to friends how he was the target of that glass of Malbec.

Preventing this kind of unfaithfulness is what inspired the Wordens to name their restaurant Piropos. Cristina is an Argentina native, and while visiting Buenos Aires with Gary many years ago a handsome man passing by said to her in Spanish, "If beauty were a sin, you'd never be forgiven." Gary, not knowing the language, asked what he'd said. Cristina explained it was a "piropo," which is Spanish for giving a woman a compliment. It's something many Argentinian men do. Gary loved the word so much that when they opened their Argentinian restaurant in Kansas City 10 years later, he suggested they name it "Piropos." In honor of the name, they've placed a list of compliments on each table for men to use on their dates—to avoid the same fate as the wine-stained wall.

The Wordens have brought the tastes, smells, and sounds of an authentic Argentinian restaurant to Kansas City. Colorful artwork from Argentina adorns the walls. Large windows allow visitors to

Left: *Peppercorn encrusted filet in brandy cream sauce.*

Top center: *Owners Gary and Cristina Worden.*

Bottom center: *The recipes derive from Cristina's Argentinian roots.*

Top right: *Homemade empanadas are a specialty.*

Bottom right: *The views from inside the restaurant are breathtaking. All images courtesy Piropos*

take in the beautiful city skyline. The crowd is loud, and the menu is diverse, with fresh handmade empanadas made according to Cristina's family's recipe. Many of the spices, salts, cheeses, and wines are imported from Argentina. The combined effect helps customers feel as if they're dining in Buenos Aires whenever they eat at Piropos.

4141 N Mulberry Dr., Kansas City, MO, 816-741-3600
piroposkc.com

The wine stain on the wall tends to fade over time, so occasionally Gary–for storytelling purposes only–will "restore" the red stain with an unfinished glass of Malbec.

JONES BBQ

Two sisters keep their "Eye" on barbecue fame

The Jones sisters have been smoking meat in Kansas City, Kansas, for a long time, but it wasn't until the Netflix show *Queer Eye* visited that their business exploded in popularity.

While in Kansas City for Season 3 of the show, the Fab Five set their sights on the Jones Sisters, who are breaking barriers as Black female pitmasters. They gave the sisters—and their business—a makeover. They also arranged for their barbecue sauce to be sold worldwide. Since then, they can hardly keep up with the demand for their food or their sauce. They say it's a good problem to have.

Deborah and Mary Jones—affectionately called "Little" and "Shorty" by family and friends—learned the art of barbecue from their father. As young girls in the early 1970s, they would stand on milk crates to stare at the mouthwatering sausages, burnt ends, and ribs their father cooked over hickory wood in the barbecue pit. To sell his meats, Leavey B. Jones Sr. took a unique approach. He stood at the corner with a checkered flag and waved cars down. He'd give them a sample of his food and if they loved it, he'd tell them to come back and buy some. If they didn't like it, he'd say, "That's all right. You can go on your way now."

Leavey taught his daughters how to cook, and eventually Little and Shorty took over his business. For years they sold their food out of a cramped taco hut, until the Fab Five came in and redesigned

> When *Queer Eye* renovated the Jones sister's restaurant, they used a black and white theme in honor of their father's checkered flag.

Left: *Like their father before them, the Jones sisters smoke meat in a barbecue pit.*
Center: *The guys from Queer Eye remodeled their old building, giving it a fresh look.*
Top right: *Owners Deborah and Mary Jones.*
Bottom right: *A plate of ribs. All images courtesy Jones BBQ*

their space. They reconfigured the kitchen, added a storefront, and put in a patio. They even offered to buy them a new oven, but the sisters refused. They had been using the same pit as their dad to smoke meat their entire lives and weren't about to change.

The Jones sisters credit their father for their success. They still wake up early each morning to cook their meats the way their father did it. They have, however, made some adjustments to the rubs and sauce. Thanks to the attention they've received on *Queer Eye* and from celebrities like Steve Harvey and Ellen DeGeneres, they've sold more than 70,000 bottles of it all around the world. These sisters continue to break barriers, feeding many of the same people their father did when he first started more than 50 years ago.

6706 Kaw Dr., Kansas City, KS, 913-788-5005
jonesbbqkc.com

CITY MARKET

A hub for all things local

There's no better place to go for great-tasting food than the City Market downtown. It's Kansas City's oldest continuously operating business. Dozens of farmers rent stalls to sell their freshly grown produce on weekends. Local restaurateurs offer unique dishes from their small shops set up around the square. You can try Ethiopian food at the Blue Nile Café, enjoy authentic Vietnamese cuisine at Hien Vuong, or visit one of the other small restaurants serving Indian, French, Cajun, Brazilian, and Middle Eastern dishes. It's a melting pot of ethnic cuisine all in one place in the center of the city.

The City Market formed in 1857, when leaders from the Town of Kansas leased the land to Jacob and Fred Scheibel for $50 a year. They turned it into a marketplace. Located by the Missouri River where the steamboats docked, the City Market became a stopping-off point for all those traveling west. Merchants sold their wares to anyone passing through. Famous customers included the likes of Wyatt Earp, Buffalo Bill Cody, and Jesse James. It became the place to go for horse-trading, political rallies, medicine shows, and circuses. City leaders decided to build downtown to the south, and over time the city began to spread out. As new options became available, people stopped visiting the City Market. It became neglected and aged. While farmers still sold produce on the weekends, it wasn't used for much else.

> Farmers markets typically run from March through October. Not at the City Market. Farmers there sell produce on weekends all year-round.

Top left: *On weekends, local farmers set up tables to sell their produce.*

Bottom left: *City Market in the early 1900s.*

Top right: *A massive sign greets you with the Kansas City skyline behind it.*

Bottom right: *Besides produce, there are dozens of mom-and-pop eateries serving all kinds of cultural cuisine.*

The City Market languished until the late 1980s, when Kansas City officials decided to invest millions of dollars to rebuild it. They brought in restaurants, retail stores, and the Steamboat Arabia Museum to attract more people to visit. Now hundreds of thousands of people visit each year. The City Market has received numerous awards and accolades from national publications for its unique approach to local commerce. Everything sold is local, and residents and visitors alike enjoy walking around the square trying new foods. Now that the streetcar goes right by it, it's easier than ever for people to visit. Today there are 180 outdoor stalls and more than 30 permanent vendors at the City Market, helping this part of Kansas City history thrive.

20 E 5th St., Kansas City, MO, 816-842-1271
thecitymarketkc.org

TOWN TOPIC

An authentic diner experience

At Town Topic Hamburgers you can step back in time, if only for a little while.

That slogan says it all. The little white diner in downtown Kansas City looks exactly as it did when it first opened more than 85 years ago. Back in 1937, Claude Sparks began selling hamburgers out of a small, iconic-looking building at 24th and Broadway. He charged 5-cents a burger, and at the end of his first day he pocketed a whopping $21—big bucks back in those days. Demand for his hamburgers grew, and in the 1950s and 1960s, he expanded, opening a total of seven locations—mostly along trolley and streetcar stops.

Claude's son, Gary, worked alongside him and took over the business when Claude passed away. Gary's son, Scott, also worked alongside his dad and eventually bought the business. His grandfather and father refused to change anything about the restaurant, and so does Scott, so the restaurant looks the same as it did in 1937. The food is made on a flatiron grill and cooked to order in front of you. He uses the burger recipe passed down from his grandfather. The fresh ground beef comes from a local supplier and is flattened on the grill with onions smashed into it, caramelizing as it cooks. You can order a single, double, triple, or bigger, and you can dress it however you want. Want eggs, hash browns, and jalapeños on it? Just ask. They'll stuff it in between a steamed bun, and you can either eat it while sitting in the old-school diner or take home a bagful.

The rest of the menu hasn't changed much, either. They still sell hand-dipped milkshakes, homemade chili, and pie that's made fresh daily. Every meal is served with a side of nostalgia. More than half of the customers are regulars who've been coming here

Top left: *Founder Claude Sparks stands behind the counter. Courtesy Town Topic*

Bottom left: *The breakfast menu hasn't changed since 1937. Courtesy Town Topic*

Bottom center: *The burger patties are mixed with onions and smashed on the grill. Courtesy Town Topic*

Top right: *Finish your meal with a slice of homemade blueberry pie and ice cream. Courtesy Town Topic*

Bottom right: *The two downtown locations are small and look the same as when they first opened.*

for years. They'll entertain you with stories of all the people who've passed through. Many grandparents also bring their grandchildren to experience this classic eatery they enjoyed as kids. It's an authentic American diner, and every time you visit you truly do feel as if you are stepping back in time—if only for a little while.

2021 Broadway Blvd., Kansas City, MO, 816-842-2298
towntopic.com

It can get a little cramped inside the diner. They only have seating for around 12 people total. If it's full, you can try the other Town Topic downtown located on 19th and Baltimore. It's literally three blocks away.

CAFÉ GRATITUDE

Where vegans go to be grateful

"**W**hat are you grateful for?"

That is the quote on the bottom of every plate of food served at Café Gratitude. Eating here is an opportunity to nourish your body and your soul. It says so in their mission statement in big, bold letters on the wall behind the bar, which contains transcendental phrases like "our food and people are a celebration of our aliveness," "honor the earth and ourselves, as we are one and the same," and "our food is prepared with love."

Michael and Natalie George brought this vegan eatery to Kansas City back in 2012. They'd eaten at a similar restaurant in California and loved the idea of opening an all-organic restaurant. To gain the right to use the name Café Gratitude, they first had to prove they could run the store with integrity. Their business philosophy is called sacred commerce, and the idea is for business to be a pathway to awakening. The Georges found the perfect location inside an old brick building in the Crossroads and renovated the space, hanging artwork to create a sense of peace and tranquility. Before every shift, the employees have a Clearing Conversation where they get all their burdens off their chest so that they can work with a clear mind.

Everything on the menu is not only organic but also plant-based. The only things not made from scratch are the bread and tortillas. Everything else is "prepared with love" in the kitchen.

> Customers can pay it forward with the Grateful Bowl. A small donation allows someone poor and hungry to get a free bowl of kale, rice, beans, and garlic tahini sauce.

Top left: *Customers are encouraged to find tranquility while eating the plant-based food.*

Bottom left: *Every plate asks, "What are you grateful for?"*

Bottom center: *The I Am Grounded appetizer consists of garlic roasted potatoes topped with a spicy cashew nacho cheese.*

Right: *Every dish starts with the words "I Am" and ends with an adjective to encourage personal reflection.*

Every dish they serve has a name that begins with the phrase "I am" and ends with an adjective related to the feeling they want you to have after eating it. For instance, the I Am Zesty is baked cauliflower bites dipped in buffalo sauce. The I Am Happy is a ciabatta bread sandwich filled with cashew cheddar, olive spread, spring greens, tomato, onion, and dill pickles. The I Am Sensational is a spaghetti squash alfredo. Their desserts are also all plant-based, and they use sea moss to keep them stable and in solid form.

You can also get a juice cleanse like the I Am Enlivened, a blue-green algae shot, or the I Am Elevated, a rose water lemonade. There are all kinds of new flavors here, and it all tastes so great that you'll leave saying, "I am grateful for…Café Gratitude."

333 Southwest Blvd., Kansas City, MO, 816-474-5683
cafegratitudekc.com

ROZZELLE COURT AT THE NELSON-ATKINS MUSEUM

Artful cuisine in an Italian courtyard

Kansas City is called the City of Fountains. There are more than 200 fountains flowing all over the city, and the oldest of these can be found inside the cafe at the Nelson-Atkins Museum. It's more than 1,800 years old, and it still works!

The iconic fountain sits in the center of Rozzelle Court, which was named after Frank Rozzelle, a donor who helped fund the construction of the original museum. When it first arrived in the mid-1930s, the fountain served as the centerpiece of an open-air courtyard. It was made back in 220 A.D. for Emperor Hadrian's villa outside Rome. Artisans carved the fountain's four-ton basin from a single piece of Cipollino marble. Over time, the fountain fell into disrepair and was found in pieces during the Renaissance. Another artisan repaired it and installed it in another villa near Rome. It sat there until 1933, when the Nelson-Atkins Museum bought it and brought it to Kansas City. They placed the bowl on the stone lion's paws, with water streaming from eight center nozzles and overflowing into a lower bowl of brownstone.

Wanting to give the courtyard a Renaissance feel, the museum put walls, columns, and arches made of pink and yellow Mankato marble around the fountain. Guests felt as if they'd stepped back in time to 15th-century Italy and would often eat a picnic lunch outside on the soft grass next to the beautiful fountain. The courtyard, though, didn't have a roof, so guests rarely used it during the hot summer and cold winter months. Forty years later, in 1974, the museum finally built a roof, but not just any roof—it's an art museum, after all. They installed a vaulted ceiling, and artist Daniel

Left: *Column arches decorate the interior of the café.*

Top center: *Sweet chile glazed salmon with wild rice and sauteed haricot verts.*

Bottom center: *The Nelson Chicken Salad with strawberry vinaigrette.*

Right: *Frank Rozzelle. All images courtesy Nelson-Atkins Museum*

MacMorris decorated it with unique paintings in the ancient Roman style. Once the roof was completed, the museum turned the space into a restaurant. No more picnic lunches. Patrons could now buy food in between looking at art.

Speaking of that food, the culinary creations are works of art. The chefs use only fresh ingredients to craft signature salads, sandwiches, soups, breads, and desserts. One of the most popular dishes is the Nelson Chicken Salad, and you can eat it in a 15th-century Italian courtyard while enjoying the sound of water gently falling from an 1,800-year-old marble fountain.

701 Grand Boulevard, Kansas City, MO, (816)221-4088
Kcanthonysongrand.com

Anthony's is part of the KC Originals, a non-profit group made up of locally owned businesses that support each other and the community through different initiatives to help feed the hungry. More than 30 restaurants take part. Learn more at kcoriginals.com

ANTHONY'S RESTAURANT & LOUNGE

Two brothers keep a family tradition alive

In 1978, Anthony Spino Jr. decided to open an Italian restaurant in downtown Kansas City. Don't do it, his friends said. It'll never last. Downtown KC is dying. No one will come. But Anthony believed in the future of the area on Grand and took a risk. And it paid off. More than four decades later, his family restaurant is still going strong. He's no longer running it. His two sons are, and it's a family affair that spans three generations.

Back in the 1960s, Anthony's parents opened a restaurant in that same space called The Soup House. They served lunch and hot soup to those who worked downtown during the day. In 1978, they handed the keys to the building to Anthony Jr. and his wife. They built an addition for extra dining space and transformed it into a traditional Italian restaurant. Anthony Jr. used his mother's family recipes from Sicily, baking fresh lasagna every morning with sweet ricotta, fresh Romano cheese, and sugo, the family's signature tomato sauce. They created a quiet, comfortable space where customers could relax and eat great-tasting food. Thanks to returning customers and word of mouth, Anthony's has been able to thrive for more than four decades.

Anthony eventually got tired of running the restaurant and handed the keys over to his two sons, Anthony III and Vito. They both added their own little touches. Every Sunday, they fry chicken and sell out nearly every week. They also added vegan, vegetarian and gluten-free options to their menu.

Anthony III met his wife at the restaurant. Her parents were regular customers. They've since moved to New York City, where

Top left: *They offer up all kinds of specials at Anthony's like shrimp scampi on a bed of noodles.*

Bottom left: *In the 1960's, Anthony Spino served soup and sandwiches in The Soup House before his son turned it into an Italian restaurant.*

Right: *Co-owners Vito and Anthony Spino III. All images courtesy Anthony's*

they run an Italian restaurant called Anthony's Eastside and offer the same family recipes but made from plant-based ingredients. Vito continues to run the Kansas City location. They are both very glad their father invested in downtown Kansas City during a down time. It paid off as today their restaurant is a Kansas City institution.

701 Grand Boulevard, Kansas City, MO, (816)221-4088
Kcanthonysongrand.com

Anthony's is part of the KC Originals, a non-profit group made up of locally owned businesses that support each other and the community through different initiatives to help feed the hungry. More than 30 restaurants take part. Learn more at kcoriginals.com

SPIN! PIZZA

How a unique pizza paved the way for copycats

First came the bagels, then the pizza.

In 1985, when the bagel craze had taken hold of the country, Gail and Richard Lozoff and their partner, Ed Brownell, founded Bagel & Bagel in Kansas City. It became so successful that they sold it to Einstein Bros. for millions of dollars and then split up. Ed moved to New York, and Gail and Richard stayed here. But after 9/11, Ed decided to move back to Kansas City. While going out to eat one night, he randomly ran into Gail and Richard. They started catching up and realized they were all interested in starting a new, unique pizza company. They put their minds and money together to create SPIN! Neapolitan Pizza.

How did the name come about? SPIN! refers to the tossing of the dough. Neapolitan is a style of pizza from Naples, Italy. In 2005, not many restaurants sold this type of pizza, where the dough is kneaded by hand and baked in a wood-fired oven. They hired award-winning chef Michael Smith to create some original recipes and used fancy Italian names to describe their pizzas. They melded fast casual with full service by having customers order and pay up front before sitting down and letting waiters handle the rest of their needs. Their concept took off. They quickly expanded, opening new SPIN! pizzerias throughout the metro area as well as in Texas, California, and Nebraska.

> SPIN! created a Kindness Program for local elementary schools. If a teacher sees a child being kind, they can reward them with a wooden token for a free pizza, drink, and gelato.

Top left: *You can order all kinds of unique pizzas, like the Roasted Potato.*

Bottom left: *The Mini Mia combo includes a 7" pizza and a soup or salad.*

Top right: *Besides pizza, they also offer tasty salads like the Superfood Salmon.*

Bottom right: *A small cup of gelato is the perfect end to a delicious meal. All images courtesy SPIN! Pizza*

Since then, many other pizzerias have opened with a similar concept. Wanting to be better than the rest, Ed polled customers and made some major changes. He took the word "Neapolitan" out of the name but kept the recipes the same. He got rid of the complicated Italian pizza names and made them simpler. He added unique pizza flavors. While the classic Margherita with basil is still on the menu, you can now order a sausage and apple pizza, a chicken pesto pizza, or a sausage and prosciutto with fig marmalade pizza. Most of their ingredients come from local vendors, and they roast and chop the toppings daily. Besides pizza, they also sell meatballs, salads, and deli sandwiches. And as for dessert, don't forget the gelato! They offer many flavors of Italian ice cream for a perfect end to your tasty, Naples-inspired meal.

6541 W 119th St., Overland Park, KS, 913-451-7746
spinpizza.com

FOX AND PEARL

Adventurous eating in a cool space

It used to be a Swedish lodge, and then a drugstore. Now it's a Midwestern bistro.

The handsome brick building occupied by Fox and Pearl has served many purposes. It was built in 1907 in the historic Westside neighborhood as a place for Swedish immigrants to gather, and owner Chef Vaughn Good and his partner, Kristine Hull, fell in love with the unique space at first sight. While it took a lot of effort to restore it to its former glory, there are now four areas where customers can eat, each different in its look and feel.

In the kitchen area, you can watch Vaughn cook from an antique farmhouse table where natural light from massive windows floods the space. The bar area features high ceilings and white marble bistro-style tabletops. The outdoor patio features a wisteria vine-covered trellis. And a spiral staircase leads down to the cellar area, where you will find an old speakeasy-style bar with velvet booths.

Vaughn grew up in Lawrence, Kansas, and after training as a chef at the International Culinary Center, he returned to his hometown in 2014 to open a butcher shop in an old gas station on Massachusetts Street. He and Kristine then turned the space into a restaurant. Since many of their customers came from Kansas City, they decided to move to Kansas City's Westside, and in 2019, they opened their new concept inside the old Swedish lodge.

Vaughn works with local farmers to source the finest meat and produce. He uses techniques like coal-roasting, hot/cold smoking, pickling, and fermenting to create memorable flavors. His menu offers one-of-a-kind delicacies like Smoked Pig Head and Chicken Liver Boudin, Smoked Pork Shank Agnolotti, and Creole

Left: *Owner Vaughn Good.*

Center: *The food is cooked in a variety of ways, sometimes over a wood fire, other times over coals.*

Top right: *In the main dining room, you can watch Vaughn cook your meal.*

Bottom right: *You might not know how to pronounce your meal, but each bite is filled with amazing flavors. All images courtesy Fox and Pearl*

Smoked Quail. Don't know what any of those things are? Just trust Vaughn's adventurous cooking methods. His culinary skills led to a nomination for Best Chef in the Midwest by the James Beard Foundation while *Esquire* named Fox and Pearl one of the 23 Best New Restaurants in America.

By the way, if you're wondering about the name, Fox and Pearl are the middle names of Vaughn and Kristine's two daughters. It truly is a family affair, as this restaurant has tapped into the pulse of this historic neighborhood, serving great-tasting food in a unique space.

2143 Summit St., Kansas City, MO, 816-437-7001
foxandpearlkc.com

The dinner and brunch menus change often, but one dish always remains on the menu—Vaughn's uber-popular Fried Chicken fermented in hot sauce and house-made pickles.

CHICKEN N PICKLE

A taste for fun games with friends

The word pickle in the name Chicken N Pickle isn't a reference to the small cucumber preserved in brine you get as a side with your meal. Sure, they give out plenty of pickles. But in this case, the word pickle stands for pickleball.

In 2015, Dave Johnson flew to Phoenix, Arizona, to visit a friend. While there, his friend introduced him to a new game called pickleball that was gaining popularity. Fascinated, Dave learned how to play this combination of tennis, badminton, and ping pong. He loved the friendly competition and the way so many who arrived as strangers left with new, lasting friendships.

Dave returned to Kansas City with an idea: he wanted to open a restaurant that offered this fun game. But Dave had no experience running an eatery. This tax manager and investor didn't let his inexperience stop him. He saw potential in this new concept and had the funds to build it, so he decided to go all in.

He built his first Chicken N Pickle in a run-down part of North Kansas City. He bought a dilapidated warehouse, tore it down, and installed indoor and outdoor pickleball courts in its place. Many friends thought he would lose money because of the location, but the opposite happened. Thousands of people flocked to his restaurant, and they often returned for more. Since opening, his concept has become so popular he's expanded into Oklahoma, Texas, and Kansas.

As for why he decided to highlight chicken on his menu, it's because one of Dave's favorite restaurants is in the Grand Cayman Islands and is called "Chicken! Chicken!" They roast their chicken over a wood fire. To replicate that flavor and quality, Dave recruited a local chef to perfect the wood-roasted style of rotisserie chicken.

Left: *Owner Dave Johnson.*

Top center: *If you want to play pickleball, reserve a court early because they go fast.*

Bottom center: *Every type of chicken sandwich comes with a pickle on the side.*

Top right: *The flavorful chicken recipes originate from the Caribbean.*

Bottom right: *All the chicken is roasted over a wood fire. All images courtesy Chicken N Pickle*

They use four different seasonings to give it a Caribbean taste. They also only serve free-range chickens that are hormone- and antibiotic-free.

As pickleball becomes more popular, many are copying Dave's idea. But Dave is trying to stay one step ahead of them. He has plans to build more of these concepts all over the Midwest, proud to offer people food and games all in the same place.

1761 Burlington St., North Kansas City, MO, 816-537-1400
chickennpickle.com

The Chicken N Pickle Foundation is a 501(c)(3) organization that partners with local charities. Dave hosts charity events at his restaurants and encourages his employees to give back, either financially or through service.

GATES BAR-B-Q

Opening the gates to great barbecue in KC

It's an iconic name, and one that many associate with the best barbecue in Kansas City. But 75 years ago, no one knew the name George Gates. He was working for the railroad while dreaming of owning a restaurant. He and his wife pooled their resources, and in 1946, they bought the Ol' Kentucky Bar-B-Q restaurant at 19th and Vine from Arthur Pinkard.

Pinkard had been an apprentice to Henry Perry, the godfather of Kansas City barbecue. Perry was the first to open a barbecue restaurant in Kansas City, and after he died in 1940, Pinkard opened Ol' Kentucky Bar-B-Q. Six years later, Pinkard wanted out. But as part of the sale, he agreed to teach George and his son, Ollie, all of Perry's famous recipes.

Perry believed there was only one right way to barbecue—in a pit with three stages. So, that's what George and Ollie did. They only changed the sauce to a tomato base and added some secret spices to better complement the meat. In 1951, a fire destroyed their restaurant. They moved to a new location and re-opened with a new name: Gates & Sons Bar-B-Q.

Ollie became instrumental in helping his father expand their barbecue empire. He spent his childhood at the restaurant and then went to college to earn a construction degree. After graduation, he put his new degree to good use. Ollie built his own barbecue restaurant at 31st and Indiana with a newly designed oven. He changed the way customers ordered food and added an iconic red roof to his restaurant. These changes improved the customer experience, and demand for his tasty barbecue grew. His family opened two more restaurants in Kansas City and even began selling their barbecue sauce in stores—which proved to be a brilliant idea.

Left: *The Struttin' Man.*

Top center: *Founder George Gates and wife Arzelia standing outside their first restaurant.*

Bottom center: *The recipes come from Henry Perry, who is considered the godfather of KC barbeque.*

Top right: *If you want ribs, be ready to order them right after an employee asks, "Hi, may I help you?"*

Bottom right: *Gates sauce is sold in stores around the world. All images courtesy Gates Bar-B-Q*

From 1975 to 1983, sales of their sauce exploded in grocery stores across the country and around the world.

There are now six Gates Bar-B-Q restaurants in Kansas City. While Ollie credits their great-tasting barbecue, he also points to a simple act of kindness. Whenever a customer walks in, an employee greets them with their signature greeting: "Hi, may I help you?" And you'd better answer right away so as not to hold up the line!

1221 Brooklyn Ave., Kansas City, MO, 816-483-3880
gatesbbq.com

> The Gates logo shows a man wearing a top hat and tuxedo. Called the "Struttin Man," it was inspired by the 1927 Louis Armstrong song "Struttin' with Some Barbecue."

MUGS UP

Freshly made root beer and a side of nostalgia

There's only one place in the metro still serving Zip Burgers, Whiz Burgers, Black Cows, and Orangaroos: Mugs Up.

This fast-food joint is frozen in time. Carhops still come to your car and take your order. They bring your food on a tray and clip it to your window. They use a change belt to give you back your change. The root beer is made fresh every day, and the loose meat sandwiches are cooked the same as they were back in 1956, when Jim and Gloria Heavey opened their first Mugs Up at 63rd and Raytown Road. It became so popular so fast that they decided to franchise. At one time, there were more than 60 Mugs Up restaurants in the Midwest. But over time many of them closed, and today there are only two left. The one in Columbia, Missouri, is only open half the year. The one in Independence is open year-round.

Ann Hinojosa bought the Mugs Up in Independence from a franchisee in 1979. Newly divorced, the realtor wanted to live closer to her girls' private school. As she perused the real estate market, she noticed a Mugs Up for sale. She remembered eating there with her grandparents as a kid, and nostalgia for those moments convinced her to buy it. But now, instead of buying fresh root beer, she was making it. Every morning, her employees dump 40-pounds of sugar into two 55-gallon refrigerated tanks and mix it with water and root beer extract. It tastes so good they often sell out by the end of the day. The price also helps. She only charges $1.25 for a large. Ann wants her food to be affordable for everyone.

Besides root beer, she sells Zip Burgers—loose meat sandwiches with pickles, onions, and mustard. The Whiz Burger is the same but with cheese. The Black Cow is a root beer float, and the Orangaroo is an orange soda float. They don't make the orange

Top left: *One of the original Mugs Up restaurants. Courtesy Mugs Up*

Bottom left: *This is the only year-round Mugs Up store still open today.*

Top right: *The root beer is made fresh every morning using a secret recipe.*

Bottom right: *The Whiz Burger is loose meat with cheese.*

soda—that comes from Polly's Pop, a local soda maker. Ann also takes pride in her chili, which comes from her own family's recipe.

Ann's Mugs Up is the last one standing in the metro area, and she is determined to stay open so people young and old can experience what eating out was like in the 1950s.

700 E 23rd St. S, Independence, MO, 816-254-7040

In 1978, Independence widened 23rd Street and forced the previous owners to move the restaurant back. They dug a basement, brought in a crane, and lifted Mugs Up to its new foundation. Instead of facing south, the entrance now faces east.

RUBY JEAN'S JUICERY

Honoring a grandmother's legacy

When Ruby Jean died in 1999, it rocked Chris Goode's world. Chris was 14 and loved his grandmother with all his heart. She helped raise him and showed her love by cooking him great-tasting soul food like raisin and sweet potato pies and cornbread. After her death, he vowed to someday honor her. He just didn't know how.

After graduating college, Chris began traveling the country for his job, and friends that he visited in L.A. introduced him to juicing. They showed him the documentary *Fat, Sick and Nearly Dead*, and it opened his eyes to the power of healthy eating. At first, Chris thought the whole juicing craze was weird. But after undergoing a 10-day juice cleanse, he felt better than ever. As he started visiting juice bars during his travels, he finally figured out how to best honor his grandmother. Because he believes Ruby Jean's soul food diet gave her diabetes, kidney disease, and high blood pressure, Chris decided he would introduce cold-pressed juices and healthier food options to the inner city, where there is little access to healthy foods. He hoped to improve people's health and maybe even save their lives.

In 2015, Chris opened his first juice bar in the lobby of a gym in Westport and named it after his grandmother. Before long, it became the most popular juice bar in Kansas City. He has since moved it into a bigger space at 30th and Troost, making it the first-ever healthy food establishment on Kansas City's east side. His best seller, Vine Street Greens, is made with red and green apples, spinach, cucumber, ginger, pineapple, lime, and kale. A Few Too Many contains grapefruit, lime, pineapple, and watermelon along with beets and ginger. Besides the juices, he also offers smoothies and protein drinks, all made with healthy ingredients.

Top left: *Ruby's face decorates the inside of the juicery.*
Bottom left: *You can order all kinds of colorful, healthy smoothies.*
Center: *Owner Chris Goode. Courtesy Ruby Jean's Juicery*
Right: *Grab a juice to go with flavors like Sunset, Vine Street Greens, and ABC.*

Chris says the secret of his success is in his slogan: *We make juice for a reason.* He doesn't just say it—he lives it. Chris donates his time and resources to local charities. He has spearheaded a "fresh juice program" to provide juices to kids in Kansas City public schools. He hires a diverse staff, many of whom need a second chance. He believes his dedication to improving the lives of others would make his late grandmother proud.

3000 Troost Ave., Kansas City, MO, 816-321-1440
rubyjeansjuicery.com

Chris is expanding his concept outside the inner city. The Missouri State grad has opened juice bars in both Springfield and Leawood as well as inside a Whole Foods Store in Brookside.

BONITO MICHOACÁN

A grocery serves up some of the best tacos in the country

They call it the Taco Trail. It's a collection of 50+ restaurants in Kansas City, Kansas, that cook up authentic Mexican food, and they serve flavorful, savory dishes many Mexicans grew up eating in their native country. *Forbes* magazine is so impressed with the quality of Mexican food here that their writers call it the best Mexican food in the country! And out of all those restaurants on the Taco Trail, only one takes the title of most unique: Bonito Michoacán.

Back in November of 2007, Armando Romero and his wife, Mayra Piñeda, moved to KCK with expansion on their minds. They had opened a small grocery store-restaurant in Houston called Bonito Michoacán. Bonito means beautiful in Spanish, and Michoacán is the name of the Mexican state where they grew up. Mayra's brother lived in KCK and convinced them to open a similar concept here. The growing Hispanic population didn't have a store where they could buy the food they ate back in Mexico, so Armando and Mayra bought a former automotive store on a deserted street and transformed it into a Mexican food paradise. The grocery-restaurant sits on one side of the street, and the Bonito Michoacán Bakery is on the other. That's where they sell flan, bolillo (Mexican French bread), and orejas (a flaky Mexican pastry). Next to that is a building called La Neña Tortilleria-Rostoseria,

> Besides the stores, Armando owns two Mexican restaurants called K-Macho. The original K-Macho is in a renovated pool hall and sits next door to the Bonito Michoacán in Olathe.

Left: *One side is a Mexican grocery while the other is an authentic Mexican restaurant.*

Top center: *The recipes come from Armando's mother, who grew up in Mexico.*

Bottom center: *Owners Armando and Mayra Pineda. Courtesy K-Macho's*

Top right: *The menudo is a great cure for hangovers.*

Bottom right: *These are some of the best tacos you will find on the KCK Taco Trail.*

where they make fresh tortillas and roasted chicken. Hispanic families from as far as Branson and Omaha flock to this grocery store/bakery/tortilla shop to get authentic Mexican products.

As for the restaurant inside the grocery, they serve tacos in a variety of meats and colors, as authentic as any you'll find in the United States. Customers rave about the parrillada (the sausage and marinated rib ends) and the menudo (a soup made from a cow's stomach that is great for curing hangovers). Every recipe originates from Armando's mother, who grew up in Mexico and learned how to cook from her own mother. It's now comfort food for Mexicans thousands of miles away from their homeland. The demand is such that they've opened another Bonito Michoacán in Olathe, plus several others in Texas. And the best part? All their stores are managed by relatives so they can keep their businesses in the family.

1150 Minnesota Ave., Kansas City, KS, 913-371-0326
bonitomichoacanmarket.com
For more on the Taco Trail: visitkansascitykc.com

CAFÉ CÀ PHÊ

Trading a Broadway career for a life in coffee

Jackie Nguyen has sung on stages all over the world. She's visited hundreds of cities. But in December of 2019, while performing on the Broadway tour of Miss Saigon, Jackie fell in love—not with a man, but with our city. She visited the Plaza lights. She experienced the River Market. Something about Kansas City called to her. When she decided to end her Broadway career and open a Vietnamese coffee truck, she knew this was the perfect place to do it.

Jackie has no ties to Kansas City. The daughter of a Vietnamese refugee, Jackie grew up in San Diego and fell in love with the stage. After college, she moved to New York to chase her dreams, working as a barista while auditioning for shows. Directors fell in love with her talent and cast her in 10 national and international tours, which gave her an opportunity to perform on Broadway and travel the world.

While visiting Vietnam, she learned about the important role her native country plays in the coffee culture. Vietnam is the second-largest exporter of coffee beans after Brazil, and not a lot of people know it. She discovered that the bean makes the difference. While most coffee-growing countries raise arabica beans, Vietnam grows robusta beans. Robusta beans contain a bolder, smoother flavor with notes of chocolate and nuts. They contain less sugar and more caffeine. Many American coffee brewers like Folgers and Maxwell House use Vietnamese beans in their blends but don't advertise it. Jackie aimed to change that.

In October of 2020, Jackie moved to Kansas City and bought a food truck. She painted a colorful dragon on it and began serving Vietnamese coffee drinks all over town. Most of her drinks are on ice since that's how most in Vietnam drink their coffee.

Left: *Owner Jackie Nguyen. Courtesy Café Cà Phê*

Top right: *When she first started, Jackie planted her trailer in different places around town to grow her customer base.*

Bottom center: *The trailer is painted like a dragon. Courtesy Café Café Cà Phê*

Bottom right: *Robusta beans from Vietnam contain less sugar and more caffeine.*

Demand for Jackie's coffee soon outgrew the truck, and Jackie now serves coffee out of a brick-and-mortar in Columbus Park. She created a Go-Fund-Me page to raise the money needed to make the transition, and now she is an inspiration for other Asian entrepreneurs. While only 2 percent of Kansas City's population is Asian, Jackie hopes her success convinces other Asians to invest in Kansas City the same way she has.

916 E 5th St., Kansas City, MO, 816-514-7066
cafecaphe.com

> Cà Phê means coffee in Vietnamese. The trick to making it so tasty? A Phin Drip. Jackie uses a metal filter to create a slow drip to enhance the flavor of the coffee beans.

STROUD'S

Pan-fried chicken made to perfection

Some consider Stroud's to be the most famous restaurant in Kansas City. Others swear they serve the best pan-fried chicken on the planet. Ironically, Stroud's got into the chicken business by accident.

Guy and Helen Stroud opened their first restaurant at 85th and Troost in 1939, a few years after the repeal of Prohibition. Initially they served barbecue rather than chicken. But when World War II broke out and beef became rationed, they switched to pan-fried chicken. Before long they had earned a reputation for serving the best fried chicken in the city.

In 1977, the Strouds sold their restaurant to two bartenders from Kelly's Westport Inn, Jim Hogan and Mike Donegon. The new owners didn't dare mess with the recipe or the menu. Soon celebrities began visiting to eat their chicken. When Yogi Berra and the World Champion Yankees were in town, they would eat dinner there. Rush Limbaugh frequently hailed the tasty chicken on his nationally syndicated radio show. The awards started coming in, too. Stroud's is the only restaurant in Kansas City to win the coveted James Beard Award for Excellence, which is typically given to chefs. Zagat's named it one of the best restaurants in the country, and dozens of national publications and TV shows have profiled it.

In 1983, Jim, Mike, and Mike's twin brother, Dennis, decided to expand and bought Oak Ridge Manor in Kansas City North. They turned the log cabin built in 1829 into a restaurant. When the city tore down the original Stroud's location on Troost in 2006 after taking possession through eminent domain, this new location up north became Stroud's new home base.

Left: *Owner Mike Donegon at the original Stroud's.*

Top center: *Stroud's at the Oak Ridge Manor in Kansas City North.*

Bottom center: *Meals are served family-style in large bowls for all to share.*

Top right: *Some national publications rank Stroud's chicken as the best in the country.*

Bottom right: *Finish off your meal with a tasty cinnamon roll. All images courtesy Stroud's*

Stroud's is known for serving meals family style. All the food is placed in the middle of the table and you grab what you want. Best of all, your meal comes with a plate of warm, tasty cinnamon rolls that many eat before diving into the chicken.

Efforts to open other Stroud's in the metro area and elsewhere in the Midwest have not always ended with success, but one constant remains. The pan-fried chicken you eat here will be among the best you've ever had.

5410 NE Oak Ridge Dr., Kansas City, MO, 816-454-9600
stroudsrestaurant.com

Stroud's has never been secretive about their recipe. They coat their chicken in flour, salt, and pepper before frying it in the pan, saying it's "how" they cook it that makes it so good.

V'S ITALIANO RISTORANTE

Momma V's dream come true

Momma V had a dream. Back in 1963, she dreamed of selling authentic Italian pizza. But first she needed a loan. So, Vita Totta went to the Blue Ridge Bank and explained her idea of opening a pizza parlor to the loan officer. His response?

"What's pizza?"

He had no clue. Yet, she convinced him to give her a $1,000 loan, an investment that paid off a thousand times over. She and her husband, Jay, went on to create one of Kansas City's most beloved Italian experiences. Of course, their menu today includes more than just pizza. Using Vita's mother's recipes from Campobello, Italy, V's serves all kinds of food, like baked lasagna (their most popular dish), steak, fettuccine, and spaghetti and meatballs bathed in a fresh red sauce that simmers at least four hours before being served.

A copy of the original menu from 1963 is posted at the front door. A spaghetti dinner back then cost just $1.50. A beer set customers back 35-cents. Prices have risen a little since then, but it's still affordable. The taste of the food, the friendliness of the staff, and the relaxed ambiance have not changed at all. For many, V's feels like home. That's why so many people have eaten here for years. Most of the waiters—along with Momma V's family members—have worked here so long, they know the customers by name. They tend to them as they do the grapes that grow outside.

> The grapes in the arbor are concord and not good for wine. Instead, they harvest them and give them to customers to make jams and jellies, only asking they share the final product with them.

Top left: *The loan officer didn't know what pizza was but still gave Mama V the dough to open her restaurant.*

Bottom left: *The colors of Italy are painted on the massive sign outside as grape vines grow on the trellis below.*

Top right: *A plate of spaghetti today will cost you a bit more than the original price of $1.50*

Bottom right: *Founder Mama V with her family. All images courtesy V's Italiano Ristorante*

Yes, they have a grape arbor outside. When they first opened, Momma V's father, Tony Barber, planted a vine, and it now covers most of the building. Three generations of Momma V's family have run her Italiano Ristorante. While she is old enough to retire, she has no plans to leave. For her, cooking homemade Italian food is not work. It's a labor she loves sharing with others.

10819 E Hwy. 40, Independence, MO, 816-353-1241
vsrestaurant.com

CHRISTINE'S FIREHOUSE

Serving up one of the city's best pork tenderloin sandwiches

Christine Seymour has mad skills behind the bar. For years she worked as a bartender, mixing drinks with a smile, and she was so friendly and so good that she developed a cult following. Her fans went wherever she worked that night. Her reputation grew. When the owner of a struggling bar and grill in North Kansas City heard about her, he decided to recruit her.

Grant Karriker owned Firehouse, so named because he worked as a firefighter. He needed something—or someone—to help drum up business. In 2012, he hired Christine to bartend but told her she'd also need to cook meals for customers. On her first night, the bar became so packed she never made it to the kitchen—she spent the whole night mixing drinks. The next night, Grant brought in two chefs so his number-one attraction wouldn't have to leave the bar. Grant, though, wasn't cut out for the restaurant business. He sold it soon after hiring Christine. The new owner promoted Christine to general manager, and she ran everything. But he, too, didn't have his heart in it, so after a couple of years Christine bought it from him. She put her name above Firehouse, and it's been packed ever since.

Most customers order the pork tenderloin sandwich. It is arguably the biggest you'll find in the metro area. After buying the restaurant, Christine wanted a unique sandwich to get more people

> If you look up, you'll see firefighter uniforms hanging from the ceiling and fire hats on the walls. Ironically, Christine's husband works as a firefighter.

Top left: *Some call Christine's pork tenderloin the best in the Midwest.*

Bottom left: *The original owner of Firehouse was a fireman.*

Top center: *Owner Christine Seymour. Courtesy Christine Seymour*

Right: *Firefighter gear hangs from the ceiling and on the walls.*

through the door. The pork tenderloin at the time was small, so she super-sized it. She wanted it to fill an entire plate with a small bun on top. The pork tenderloin is so good that it's developed a cult following on social media. Patrons have encouraged her to enter it into a contest. Surely it would win! But Christine doesn't need or want the accolades. The smiles on the faces of the customers who eat it are good enough for her.

You won't see Christine behind the bar serving drinks anymore. She doesn't want to take away tips from her employees, and besides, she's too busy doing everything else. There are a lot of people to serve, and the pork tenderloin doesn't fry itself.

220 E 20th Ave., North Kansas City, MO, 816-255-2343

SYLAS AND MADDY'S HOMEMADE ICE CREAM

Three generations creating unique flavors together

When Jim and Cindy England opened their first ice cream shop in Lawrence, Kansas, back in 1997, they didn't name it after their kids. They named it after their pets. Sylas was their cat, and Maddy was their dog.

They got into the ice cream business by accident. Jim worked at 3M, and Cindy worked at the Gap. They both worked long hours and wanted to spend more time with their daughters. What to do? Since they had both worked at an ice cream store shortly after they were married, Cindy suggested they open one of their own. They rented a storefront in downtown Lawrence and went to work creating a tasty recipe for premium ice cream. They then enlisted their daughters to help come up with some fun flavors and creative names. Kansas Twister, Gold Dust, Maddy's Mud, and Yellow Brickle Road all give a nod to Kansas history. Unicorn Fluff, Princess Raspberry, and Queen of Hearts came from their daughters' whimsical side. And since they are located between several colleges with loyal followings, they created Rock Choc Jayhawk and The Phog for KU fans, Tiger Tracks for Mizzou fans, and Powercat Crunch for K-State fans.

The England family makes the ice cream daily using fresh ingredients. For the watermelon sorbet, they chop up an entire watermelon and mix it in. Pie-flavored ice creams get an entire pie mixed in. By their estimation, they've created more than 130 different flavors of ice cream. They also make all their waffle cones fresh daily, and those typically sell out by the end of the day.

Top left: *A small cup of ice cream will cost you $2.96. With tax, it rounds up to the nearest nickel or dime.*

Bottom left: *Customers can send in flavor ideas and if they make it, you'll be rewarded with a sweet treat.*

Top right: *Fun chalk boards on the walls explain the ice cream flavors available.*

Bottom right: *The ice cream and waffle cones are made fresh daily.*

So many people packed their parlor the first two years they decided to open a second ice cream store in Olathe, Kansas. Today, Jim and Cindy are retired and have handed off the operations of the two stores to their daughters. But they'll still go in to help make the ice cream. Best of all, their hard work with this family venture is paying off. Several publications have called their ice cream the best in Kansas, and they hope to continue bringing smiles to people's faces one sugary treat at a time.

11925 Strang Line Rd., Olathe, KS, 913-393-3500
sylasandmaddysicecream.com

The prices are very unconventional. A small cup is $2.96, a medium $3.63, and a large $4.34. Why? When you add tax, the cost rounds up to the nearest nickel or dime, so employees don't have to hand out pennies.

TAPS ON MAIN

Want a beer? Pour your own!

The Kansas City Royals played a big part in the creation of Taps on Main.

Back in 2014 and 2015, the Royals were the toast of the town. They played in two consecutive World Series, winning one in 2015. During that time, pride for Kansas City and the team swelled. Everyone wanted to watch the games at a sports bar, and it inspired many—including the Tower brothers—to invest in the local culinary and craft beer scene. Breweries and bars began popping up everywhere.

Grant Tower wanted in on this movement. He'd spent more than a decade in the restaurant business and dreamed of owning his own place. He convinced his two brothers, Jason and Marc, to combine their resources and build a sports bar downtown. They installed a bunch of TVs, gathered delicious recipes, and brought in high-quality craft beers and whiskeys. But to make it truly stand out from other bars, Grant built a 40-tap beer wall. Instead of having the bartender do the pouring, he let customers pour their own.

Here's how it works: When you walk in, they give you a card and connect it to your credit card. You then grab a glass, go to the tap wall, put your card up to whatever beer you want to try, and pour as much or as little as you want. It's a chance to try new flavors and brands before committing to a full pour. Grant and his

> Wanting to cater to health-conscious customers, Grant partners with local bakery Three Bears and serves every burger and sandwich on a zero-carb bun. You can also get fried zucchini chips as an alternative to French fries.

Left: *Owners Jason and Grant Tower. Courtesy Taps on Main*

Top center: *While the array of beers is the main draw, the chefs elevate bar food to a whole new level.*

Bottom center: *They offer vegetarian options with keto bread from Three Bears Bakery.*

Top right: *You can try all kinds of beer when you pour it yourself from the tap wall.*

Bottom right: *The wings recipe comes from the owners' father—who is from Buffalo, New York.*

staff rotate the taps often and have a great selection of local beers. You can sit on the patio, sip on your drink, and watch the game with friends while you wait for your food.

As for the food, it's won several awards for deliciousness. Besides burgers and cheesesteaks, the main draw is the Tonawanda wings. Grant's dad is from Tonawanda, New York, right outside Buffalo—where Buffalo wings were invented. He spent decades perfecting the recipe his sons now use. They're so tasty they've had customers from western New York comment that they're as good or better than anything they get back home.

By creating a fun after-work vibe and giving the power of the pour to the people, Grant and his brothers have created a unique place to watch a game while drinking something new.

1715 Main St., Kansas City, MO, 816-291-4502
tapsonmain.com

LONNIE'S RENO CLUB

Step into the 1930s with a local jazz legend

He's a triple threat whenever he steps on the stage. He can sing, dance, and play the trumpet, and you can see him do all three at Lonnie's Reno Club.

Lonnie McFadden grew up in Kansas City's Jazz District and watched his father, Jimmy, tour the country with many great jazz artists. Jimmy performed in front of sold-out crowds, and Lonnie wanted to follow in his footsteps. Jimmy taught Lonnie and his younger brother, Ronald, the tricks of the trade, and in 1974, they formed a band that their father managed. Lonnie and the Band— later renamed The McFadden Brothers—spent the next few decades entertaining crowds around the world, traveling as far as Japan. They even performed on television and shared the stage with Sammy Davis Jr., the Count Basie Orchestra, and Wayne Newton. They made a good living doing what they loved.

As Lonnie grew older, he went solo and booked gigs at restaurants and lounges in Kansas City. Then the pandemic hit. Stuck at home, unable to perform, Lonnie caught a break when Eric Willey, the manager of the Ambassador Hotel in downtown Kansas City, asked him to do a set on an outdoor stage. It went so well that Eric offered Lonnie a unique opportunity. The ballroom in the hotel's basement was not being used. Would Lonnie consider turning it into his own private nightclub? Lonnie loved the idea and wanted to create a 1930s speakeasy vibe. They built a stage, brought in plush furniture, and dimmed the lights for an intimate atmosphere. Lonnie put together a four-piece band to perform on weekends. Visitors can now walk downstairs, order a drink, eat a delicious meal, and groove to jazz as Lonnie commands the stage.

Eric put together a menu of dishes and drinks from the 1930s. For $95, you can get a three-course meal of your choice. Lonnie's

Top left: *Jazz artist Lonnie McFadden*

Bottom left: *The drinks, music, and ambiance transport you to the nightclubs of the 1930s.*

Bottom center: *The beef Wellington is a fan favorite.*

Top right: *The McFadden Brothers when they performed all over the world.*

Bottom right: *A three-course meal of your choice plus a show with Lonnie and his band will cost you $95. All images courtesy Lonnie's Reno Club*

favorite is the beef Wellington. As for drinks, they offer Prohibition favorites like the old-fashioned, Manhattan, and lemon drop. It's a one-of-a-kind experience, watching a living legend sing, tap, and play on stage. Lonnie also always takes time to walk into the crowd and shake hands, thanking the crowd for letting him share his talents with his guests and all of Kansas City.

1111 Grand Blvd., Kansas City, MO, 816-326-7897
lonniesrenoclub.com

Lonnie named his venue after the Kansas City Reno Club, where great African American jazz artists performed in the 1930s. Pictures of legendary performers like Count Basie and Charlie "Bird" Parker decorate the walls.

THE CLASSIC CUP CAFÉ

A Plaza mainstay redefines the patio brunch

If you love to people-watch, the sidewalk patio at The Classic Cup Café is the place to be.

This quaint café sits in the Country Club Plaza, which opened back in 1923. Tourists from all over the world come here to shop at dozens of high-end retailers lining 15 city blocks in the heart of Kansas City. Developed by JC Nichols with Spanish-style architecture, the Plaza was the first suburban planned shopping center in the country. The beautiful buildings and flowing fountains give the area a glamorous feel.

Customers at The Classic Cup Café get a front row seat to watch shoppers as they pass by the outdoor terrace. Putsch's Sidewalk Café used to operate out of this building, but in 1989, Dan and Charlene Welling moved their café into this space. Their Classic Cup Café in Westport, which opened in 1982, was doing so well they decided to expand. But after a few years of operating two cafés, they became overwhelmed, and in 1993, they sold their Plaza location to John Meyer. He then ran it until 2016, when he sold it to Dan McCall, one of his former managers, who continues to run it today.

While the menu has changed over the past three decades, several items have become mainstays. Customers clamor for the restaurant's signature bread; a loaf of rye, whole wheat, and white doughs. The pancakes are so popular they sell the dry mix at Hen House grocery stores. The shrimp and grits have also been on the menu since the very beginning. One of their best-loved dishes is the Migas, which is a combination of corn tortillas, eggs, chorizo, sour cream, and cheese.

Left: *The low country shrimp and grits is a favorite of many customers.*

Top right: *They serve breakfast, lunch, and brunch all day long.*

Bottom right: *The outdoor sidewalk patio is the perfect place to eat and watch people as they shop on the Plaza.*

They used to serve three meals a day to packed crowds, but after the financial crash of 2008, business began to slow. More people began to shop online, and the foot traffic at the Country Club Plaza grew thin. To survive, they decided to do away with dinner. Now, they only offer breakfast, brunch, and lunch from 8 a.m. until 2 p.m. This gives their customers a good seven hours to swing by for a nice meal on the patio, where they can continue to people-watch in this historic shopping district.

301 W 47th St., Kansas City, MO, 816-753-1840
theclassiccupcafe.com

Down five flights of stairs sits the wine cellar, a beautiful room now used as meeting space and reception hall. While they don't store wine there anymore, there are still a few bottles on the shelf for good measure.

THE FARMHOUSE

Where farm-to-table is a way of life

The Farmhouse is truly a farm-to-table operation. They grow vegetables in a garden out back, and local farmers sell them other produce and meat. The menu changes based on what's in season, and when planning what dishes to serve, they use every part of the animal. The bones are used to make broth, the fat to fry vegetables, and the meat . . . well, the meat is the best part, and it's a big reason why customers continue to come back for more.

Back in 2009, the farm-to-table concept didn't exist in Kansas City. But chef Michael Foust wanted to open a restaurant that only served the freshest food. He partnered with 30 different local farmers and opened his new concept in the River Market. He renovated one of Kansas City's oldest buildings, which used to serve as a brothel for the mob. If only the walls could talk! Right away, customers fell in love with the fresh tastes they could depend on whenever they visited. They also felt good knowing their business helped local farmers thrive.

In 2018, Foust decided to move on and sold the restaurant to three men who continue to partner with local farmers for most of their ingredients. Chef Vince Paredes took over the kitchen and brought his own style of Mexican cuisine to the table. His tamales are delicious! But the menu isn't all Mexican fare—it's

> The corned beef hash is one of the most popular dishes. When actor Hugh Jackman tried it while visiting Kansas City, he proclaimed it the best he's ever eaten. His next time in town, he took his entire crew there to try it.

Top left: *The menu changes frequently based on produce in season and what they get from local farmers.*

Bottom left: *Employees grow some of their own vegetables in a garden out back.*

Top center: *Chef Vince Paredes brings a taste of Mexico to many of his dishes.*

Bottom center: *The Farmhouse popularized the farm-to-table concept in Kansas City.*

Right: *The restaurant sits inside a former brothel run by the mob.*

a true reflection of what farmers have available. One dish that's been mainstay on the menu from the beginning is the Hanger steak. That's a cut of meat close to the tenderloin that restaurants typically don't sell. It takes a lot of manual labor to prepare it. But the chefs at The Farmhouse put in the effort since they don't want to waste any part of the animal.

Their hours are limited, so you'll want to call ahead for a reservation. They've won a lot of awards for their brunch, which is one reason why it's hard to get a table. But their biggest accomplishment is supporting local farmers by using their meat, grains, fruits, and vegetables to create a one-of-a-kind culinary experience.

300 Delaware St., Kansas City, MO, 816-569-6032
eatatthefarmhouse.com

JASPER'S MARCO POLO

Obsessed with great Italian food—and cannoli

Chef Jasper Mirable Jr. is obsessed with cannoli.

He loves the sweet treat, a classic Sicilian dessert of ricotta cheese blended with cream and sugar stuffed inside a pastry shell. In fact, he loves cannoli so much he's writing a cookbook about it. He created National Cannoli Month (it's September). And whenever he gains weight, he can trace it back to the tasty cannoli sitting on the dessert cart in his restaurant.

The cannoli is one of many desserts Jasper serves at his restaurant, which he co-owns with his brother, Leonard. They took over the family business in 1998 after their father passed away.

Jasper Mirable Sr. and his wife, Josephine, immigrated to Kansas City from Sicily. In 1954, they opened Jasper's on 75th Street in Waldo and introduced cuisine from their homeland using recipes handed down over generations. Thirty years later, the Mirables opened Marco Polo's Italian Market next door, offering customers carryout deli sandwiches and other Italian entrées. Fifteen years after that, they decided to sell their old building and build a new one in south Kansas City near 103rd and State Line Road. Jasper Sr. wanted his new restaurant to be more accessible to all. But two months before opening, he passed away, leaving Jasper Jr. and Leonard to take over the family business. They have taken up their father's mantle and continue to serve great Italian food in his memory.

Over the years, the Mirables' traditional Sicilian recipes have attracted many famous customers like then-Governor Ronald Reagan, Bob Hope, Hank Williams Jr., George Brett, Eric Stonestreet, and Paul Rudd. Old World dishes like Scampi Alla Livornese, Chicken Parmigiano, and Veal Limonata have been on the menu from the very beginning.

Top left: *The Chicken Parmigiano*

Bottom left: *Jasper is obsessed with cannoli, offering all kinds of flavors in September.*

Top center: *Jasper's has sat at 103rd and State Line since the early 1970s.*

Bottom center: *The Gondola, an original Italian meatball sandwich with mozzarella cheese and tomato sauce.*

Right: *Owner Jasper Mirable Jr. All images courtesy Jasper's Marco Polo*

Since his dad passed, Jasper Jr. has become the face of the restaurant. Besides writing cookbooks, he hosts a radio show, writes columns, sells his own brand of pasta sauce with his picture on the front, and shares his recipes on television. Jasper's Restaurant is in the Fine Dining Hall of Fame and has been named one of the best Italian restaurants in the country by numerous publications. *USA Today* calls it the best Italian restaurant in Kansas City.

By offering tasty Sicilian dishes in an upscale atmosphere, Jasper's Marco Polo allows guests to visit Italy without ever leaving their tables.

1201 W 103rd St., Kansas City, MO, 816-941-6600
jasperskc.com

In September, in honor of National Cannoli Month, Jasper features a different house-made cannoli each day with flavors like bananas foster, pumpkin spice, gooey butter cake, and cheesecake.

THE MAJESTIC RESTAURANT

A former saloon offering steak with a side of jazz

This restored piece of Kansas City history truly is majestic. But before they started serving steaks and jamming to jazz, it was a saloon and brothel.

In 1911, as the population of Kansas City began to grow, James A. Fitzpatrick opened a saloon at 10th and Broadway. He served drinks on the first floor and offered women on the second. James had a powerful friend—corrupt political boss Tom Prendergast—so when Prohibition hit, the booze didn't disappear. James simply moved his bar to the basement and turned it into a speakeasy. Jazz artists like Charlie Parker and Count Basie played all night while the liquor flowed. Prendergast provided the alcohol and used the tunnels in the basement to move booze from one speakeasy to another.

After Prohibition ended, the neighborhood transformed into the Garment District. The clothing industry boomed as businesses in the area churned out more coats and women's clothes than any other city but New York. Fitzpatrick's saloon closed and the building was repurposed as a clothing manufacturing plant. Eventually, the building was abandoned and fell into disrepair.

In 1983, two Kansas City couples saw the beauty in the old Fitzpatrick Saloon Building and decided to buy it. They spent two years restoring the old building. They polished the exterior copper façade, restored the original molded tin ceiling, and brought in a 40-foot-long bar built in 1900. They opened a steak restaurant on the first floor and put a jazz club in the basement. They also opened the Tom Prendergast Club, where members can smoke a cigar,

Top left: *You can eat a steak dinner in the basement, where they offer live jazz on many nights.*

Left: *The mural on the wall honors famous people with Missouri roots.*

Top right: *They have an extensive bar with more than 400 types of whiskeys. All images courtesy The Majestic*

drink from a collection of 400 whiskeys, and eat a perfectly cooked steak. But if you go, be prepared to pay for that great steak—prices range from $45 to $68 a cut. They are only open for dinner, and a reservation is recommended. But you can revel in the past as The Majestic continues to offer booze and music, carrying on a tradition that started more than 110 years ago.

931 Broadway Blvd., Kansas City, MO, 816-221-1888
majestickc.com

> When you walk inside, look at the front wall. The owners commissioned an original oil canvas mural from famed local artist Jack O'Hara that depicts stars with strong Kansas City ties, including Walt Disney, Charlie Parker, and Ernest Hemmingway.

STRANG HALL

Six different restaurants under one roof

They call it a chef collective. Six gourmet restaurants in the same building serving different types of food: sushi, Mexican, vegan, pizza, sandwiches, and Southeast Asian. There's something for everyone. Customers can sit at long, wooden tables or outside on the patio to enjoy a festive, communal atmosphere.

Chef Brett DeHart owns two of the eateries. Fenix serves gourmet Mexican while Tora Sushi serves sushi. Brett started cooking in his family's restaurant in Topeka at the age of 15. He loved it but wanted to carve his own path in the culinary industry. He moved to Kansas City to learn how to make different kinds of food and even apprenticed under a sushi master in Prairie Village, who nicknamed him "Tiger." When Brett moved to Salt Lake City to run a restaurant, he became homesick. He wanted his own place back home.

That's when he heard from Joe Follett.

Joe was tasked with finding chefs to run restaurants in the newly built Strang Hall. He knew Brett by reputation and knew he wanted to return to Kansas City. Joe flew out to Salt Lake City to recruit Brett. Would he rent a kitchen or two at Strang Hall? Brett didn't hesitate.

Neither did Anourom Thomson. Anourom left Laos as a child when his father snuck the family out of the country. They lived in a refugee camp for a few years, and in 1980, while his father stayed behind, his mother took the family to Kansas City. Her cooking comforted Anourom during this transition to a new country without his father. He later cut his chops at Pierpont's and Hereford House before going out on his own, serving Southeast Asian food from a food truck. When Joe asked him to be the first

Top left: *You can order a quesadilla at Fenix, the Mexican eatery.*

Bottom left: *Chef Brett DeHart was nicknamed "Tiger" by the sushi master who trained him.*

Top center: *An open floorplan allows you to explore all the restaurants, the bar, and the patio.*

Bottom center: *Sushi is offered at one of the six restaurants.*

Right: *Chef Anourom Thomson named his restaurant after his late brother. Courtesy Strang Hall*

tenant of Strang Hall, Anourom accepted. He named his restaurant Anousone in honor of his older brother, who died when they were children in Laos.

Anourom and Brett both love the relationships they've formed with each other and the other chefs. They learn from each other. They compete for customers. It makes them better. And the customers benefit. By offering a fun, communal atmosphere and food you can't get anywhere else, the chefs at Strang Hall have combined forces to create an experience everyone will enjoy.

7313 W 80th St., Overland Park, KS, 913-210-0475
stranghall.com

The owners of Strang Hall plan to build smaller Strang Halls in Kansas City, where two to three chefs–instead of five or six–will offer different tastes under the same roof.

153

CLINTON'S SODA FOUNTAIN

Step back in time and enjoy refreshing, sugary treats

Decades before becoming President and leading America out of World War II, Harry Truman swept floors and wiped down tables at Clinton's Drug Store in downtown Independence. The 14-year-old future president earned 15 cents a week. He'd come in early and stay late after school to keep the popular soda fountain clean. But his first job lasted only two weeks. His father didn't want Harry's grades to suffer, so he forced his son to quit. Afterward, Harry still visited often because they served up his favorite frozen treat: a chocolate ice cream sundae drenched in butterscotch.

You can still order Harry's Favorite at Clinton's Soda Fountain today. It's in the same building where Harry once worked, and it exudes all the warmth and charm of an early 20th-century soda fountain. The checkerboard floor, wood cabinets, and molding are all original. You can sit on a red stool in front of a 100-year-old marble countertop and order a phosphate. That's a colorful, bubbly soft drink originally created in 18th-century France. Its signature tang comes from phosphoric acid. Prefer ice cream? Order a phosphate float, a banana split with all the fixings, or a traditional ice cream sundae. Sauces range from hot fudge to caramel to marshmallow to strawberry. Besides ice cream, Clinton's only serves four types of grilled cheese sandwiches, a peanut butter and jelly sandwich, and tomato soup.

This throwback to history wouldn't be here without Ken and Cindy McClain. The original drug store closed in the early 1980s and sat empty for a few years before the McClains decided to buy the building. Instead of tearing it up and introducing a new restaurant, they restored the building and brought back an old

Left: *The 100-year-old countertop and stools are a nod to the days when soda fountains were all the rage.*

Top right: *This is one of the only places that still makes phosphates, a soft drink that originated in France.*

Bottom right: *Harry's favorite ice cream sundae is drenched with butterscotch.*

favorite. Today, this is one of the only places in the metro area—if not the only place—where you can buy a phosphate. Thanks to the McClains' efforts to preserve this piece of history, kids and adults can continue to get a sweet treat whenever they visit the historic Independence Square.

100 W Maple Ave., Independence, MO, 816-833-2046
clintonssodafountain.com

> You can buy Polly's Pop here. Created by L. L. "Polly" Compton in 1923, it was a best seller for many years until production shut down in 1967. Forty-five years later, the McClains bought the brand and now offer fun flavors like glazed donut, black cherry, pineapple, and peach.

IRON DISTRICT

Serving great food inside shipping containers

Jonelle Jones was frustrated. Physical therapy was not solving her medical issues. She tried a two-week juice cleanse and felt much better, so she and her husband Phillip decided to go vegan. Not only that but because Phillip is a trained chef with 25 years of experience, they decided to go all-in by opening a vegan restaurant.

Jonelle saw a post on social media proposing a new eating district where all the restaurants would work out of shipping containers. Wanting to start small, Jonelle answered the ad, and she and Phillip became the first tenants in the newly formed Iron District. They named their restaurant "kind food," sending a message that their way of cooking would be kind to animals, kind to the environment, and kind to people. Everything they use, from the food to the containers, is compostable—no plastic. Getting vegan food to taste good is a challenge, but Phillip was up to the task. He's created delicious-tasting vegan burgers, wraps, and nachos. That's it for entrées, although they come in a variety of flavors with different add-ons to personalize the eating experience. Instead of dairy-based cheese, he uses cashew cheese. Instead of chicken, he uses soy. His bacon isn't made of pig fat—it's made from coconut. The flavors are so fantastic that people keep coming back for more, and they eventually outgrew the container and moved into a storefront in Kansas City, Kansas. Their success is a big reason why many other chefs are setting up shop in the Iron District.

> Phillip donates all his leftover food to an organization called Food, Not Bombs. They give it to the hungry and homeless. He also donates a percentage of the profits to different charities to live up to the word "kind" in their name.

Top left: *The restaurants and stores work in shipping containers arranged with a seating area in the middle.*

Bottom left: *Nachos are just one of the many types of food you can get in the Iron District.*

Top right: *kind food Owner Phillip Jones. His eatery was the first one here, and he later moved to a bigger storefront.*

Bottom right: *The kind food burger is made of beans, not meat, and the cheese from cashews, not milk.*

The original concept came from the mind of Rachel Kennedy. She and her partners bought 18 shipping containers and built kitchens inside some of them. She arranged the containers in a square with tables and games in the middle of a small courtyard. Voila! A new type of food and entertainment venue emerged. Entrepreneurs wanting to test their concepts with the public can rent a container with little risk. The rent is low, they keep all the profits, and if it doesn't work? They can get out without massive debt hanging over their heads. This incubator for startups consists of restaurants, bars, boutiques, and a bookstore. Their slogan is *Eat. Drink. Shop. Connect.* They hope that over time more aspiring startups will come to the Iron District to test their new concepts from inside a shipping container.

599 Iron St., North Kansas City, MO, 816-281-7471
irondistrictnorthkc.com

BO LING'S

Bringing the Chinese custom of dim sum to KC

Theresa never wanted to move to Kansas City. Heck, she didn't want to move to America. But in 1971, her father forced the 16-year-old and the rest of her family to emigrate from Hong Kong. He wanted a better life for his family, so they moved to New York. Theresa's father worked as a chef at a Chinese restaurant for a couple years before he moved his family to Kansas City. With virtually no Chinese community here at that time, she felt like a fish out of water. But her father opened a Chinese restaurant called The Dragon Inn, and the entire family worked nonstop to make it thrive.

A few years later, Theresa's father hired a young chef named Richard Ng. He was in the first graduating class of the new culinary program at Johnson County Community College. Richard and Theresa fell in love and married. In 1981, they decided to start their own restaurant. Theresa's father brought in an acclaimed Chinese chef from New York to teach them how to make sauces. He shared many of his own recipes. Those recipes are a big reason why Theresa and Richard's restaurant is still around more than 40 years after opening.

In 1987, Richard and Theresa introduced the Cantonese tradition of dim sum to Kansas City. It's an Asian brunch with lots of small plates of traditional Chinese food along with tea. Few Chinese restaurants offer this unique type of meal in the Midwest. People from as far away as Arkansas and Nebraska will drive to Kansas City just to experience it.

Theresa and Richard use only fresh ingredients to make every dish, sauce, and stock from scratch. Customer favorites include the steamed dumplings with homemade wrappers, moo shu pork with sliced meats and a homemade pancake, and the pineapple fried rice served in a pineapple boat.

Top: *There are six Bo Lings locations and counting.*

Bottom left: *You can eat dim sum at the restaurant and then take other dishes home to eat later.*

Bottom center: *Owners Richard and Theresa Ng.*

Bottom right: *Many of the recipes come from Theresa's father. All images courtesy Bo Ling's*

Bo Ling's has racked up some impressive awards. *USA Today* once named them one of the 10 best gourmet Chinese restaurants in the country. As demand for their delicious food increased, Richard and Theresa decided to expand. They currently own six restaurants in the metro. Three generations of Ng family members have worked at Bo Ling's. They've shared their family and Chinese culture with others for four decades, and they plan to continue doing it for many years to come.

8973 Metcalf Ave., Overland Park, KS, 913-341-1718
bolings.com

> The name "Bo Ling's" is a combination of Richard and Theresa's names. Richard's family called him Bo as a kid, which means "treasure" in Chinese. Theresa's Chinese name is Far Ling.

J. RIEGER & CO

Preserving KC's history of whiskey

A blend of history, whiskey, and beer ooze from the J. Rieger & Co. distillery.

Located in the historic Electric Park neighborhood in the East Bottoms, the beautiful brick building where J. Rieger makes sherry-infused whiskey began as a brewery. Built back in 1901, Heim Brewery bottled 100,000 bottles of beer a day out of the three-story brick building and shipped them by rail car all over the country. During that same period, Jacob Rieger distilled his fine whiskey in the West Bottoms, becoming the largest mail-order whiskey company in the country. Both booze barons prospered. But in 1920, Prohibition forced them to shut down their operations and they remained closed—until 2014.

Nearly a century after Prohibition, the great-great-great grandson of Jacob Rieger decided to resume the family business. Andy Rieger and his business partner, Ryan Maybee, built a distillery inside the old Heim Brewery. They hired a former high school teacher, Nathan Perry, to be their head distiller. They tried to duplicate Jacob Rieger's 1880s-style whiskey recipe and created a tasty spirit. Sales took off. Then they went a step further and renovated the rest of the 120-year-old building, investing millions of dollars to make it a destination for locals and tourists alike.

On the first floor sits a store where you can buy their whiskey, vodka, caffe amaro, and gin, along with shirts and other memorabilia. To the right, sits a small exhibit filled with artifacts honoring the history of whiskey and beer production in Kansas City. Through massive windows you can see the stills and machinery used in the distilling process. And to the left, you can

Left: *When renovating the old Heim Brewery, they added kitchens and hired trained chefs to make upscale food.*

Right: *Owners Andy Rieger (right) and Ryan Maybee (left) with head distiller Nathan Perry (center). All images courtesy J. Rieger & Co*

go outside to a heated patio where there is a bar and often live entertainment.

On the second floor sits the Monogram Lounge, where you can grab a cocktail and a bite to eat. Local brewery K.C. Bier created a special beer honoring the 1900 recipe Heim used, and you can only find it here. The menu combines J. Rieger spirits with fresh ingredients to create some truly unique flavors. For instance, the Heim pretzel features Heim beer cheese. The cedar roasted salmon uses Rieger's gin salt. And the whiskey-glazed baby backs are glazed with—what else—Rieger's whiskey.

Did I mention the slide? J. Rieger & Co also owns the only distillery slide in the world. So, instead of stumbling down the stairs after enjoying a few drinks, you can slide down to the front door, where your taxi awaits.

2700 Guinotte Ave., Kansas City, MO, 816-702-7800
jriegerco.com

Downstairs sits the Hey! Hey! Lounge, a throwback speakeasy where you can grab a nightcap, listen to live jazz in a plush chair, and soak in the club-like vibes channeling the early 1900s.

THE QUAFF

A historic dive bar serving the thirsty

Quaff (*v.*): to drink heartily

Quaff (*n.*): a dive bar in Kansas City that's served drinks for more than 75 years

When you go to the Quality Hill neighborhood in downtown Kansas City where The Quaff is located, it's hard to miss. Thirty neon signs shine brightly from the windows, welcoming you in. Many customers return night after night because it's their favorite place to watch sports. The staff knows their names and what they drink. Named by some publications as the best sports bar in Kansas City, The Quaff always shows local games on the dozens of big-screen TVs scattered throughout the bar.

Antonio Bonino opened this small bar the year after World War II ended. During the war, he had fought for the US against his home country of Italy and earned automatic citizenship because of it. He moved to Kansas City and opened the "1010 Club" with his best friend. They invited working-class families who lived nearby to gather there after a hard day of manual labor. He later changed it to "The Quaff" because, well, it sounded better. When the neighborhood fell on hard times in the 1970s, many families cleared out, but The Quaff persevered. In the 2000s, the city redeveloped the area and thousands of young professionals moved downtown. They are now the regulars, haunting the bar late into the night as they quaff their favorite beers and root their teams to victory.

Much of The Quaff looks as it did in 1946. The bar has a few more scratches and stains from years of wear and tear, and Antonio's grandsons and their families now run the place. Drinks are their specialty, and Crown Royal is a favorite as they sell more

Left: *Many employees have served customers here for decades and will help them get home if they drink too much.*

Top right: *Steak night brings in big crowds.*

Bottom right: *The qwaffles come tossed in a honey bourbon glaze in a small cast iron skillet.*

of that whiskey than any other bar in the state. As for food, they serve bar staples like wings, nachos, burgers, and pizza, but they also offer $13 steaks on Wednesday nights, chicken and waffles, and hearty salads. They've won many awards, including Best Dive Bar in Kansas City from *The Pitch* and the Best Late Night Hours from *USA Today*. They are open daily until 3 a.m.

So the next time you're thirsty, swing by The Quaff. Even if you don't drink heartily, you can still enjoy the friendly faces welcoming you to Kansas City's favorite dive bar.

1010 Broadway Blvd., Kansas City, MO, 816-471-1918
quaffkc.com

If you end up drinking too much—as many a customer has—the staff will walk (or carry) you home. They want their customers to be safe so they'll visit again.

THE ROASTERIE

Searching the world for the best coffee beans

Her name is Betty and she's a beauty.

Her massive wings extend over the top of the Roasterie's main headquarters and glow blue at night. During the day, the sun shines off her svelte silver body while her long propellers spark the imagination. She's a Douglas DC-3, a plane from another era, and Roasterie founder Danny O'Neill named her after his mom. This symbol of adventure is what inspired him to follow his dreams.

Danny first fell in love with coffee as a foreign exchange student in Costa Rica back in 1978. That's where he learned the art of picking coffee cherries and all the hard work it took for independent farmers to grow high-quality coffee beans. Fifteen years later, Danny's obsession with coffee inspired him to air-roast his own beans in the basement of his Brookside home. He bought the best beans directly from farmers around the world and went door-to-door to sell them.

Demand for his quality coffee grew. Danny needed a bigger factory and moved into an old building at 27th and Southwest Boulevard. He hired a staff and started flying all over the world to find the best beans, negotiating directly with small coffee bean farmers, paying above market prices to support them.

Danny decided to market his product with a picture of the DC-3, putting Betty on every bag of his coffee. For many years, exporters used this type of plane to transport coffee beans around the world. Danny even dreamed of putting a full-sized DC-3 on the roof of his building, and in 2012, he found one in an airplane junkyard. This particular plane, built in the 1930s by TWA, had been the first to fly passengers for a profit. He bought it and hired engineers to safely secure it to his building. Even though she can no longer fly, Betty overlooks the city and looks as if she is ready to takeoff once again.

Top left: *A Douglas DC-3 poised to takeoff from the top of The Roasterie factory.*

Bottom left: *"Betty," as the plane is called, graces all the marketing materials for this unique coffee shop.*

Top center: *The packaging on every bag explains where in the world your beans were grown.*

Bottom center: *You can drink a fancy coffee, see how they roast and package the beans, and try new flavors inside their factory.*

Right: *Founder Danny O'Neill. All images courtesy The Roasterie*

The café serves all types of flavors created by coffee beans bought from 31 different countries. You can also tour the factory and learn more about the unique cupping, roasting, and blending process behind their air-roasted coffee. And when you leave, you can take some coffee home with you, supporting Danny's dream of sharing the best coffee in the world with Kansas City.

1204 W 27th St., Kansas City, MO, 816-931-4000
theroasterie.com

The Roasterie runs a Barista Training Academy where students work with skilled roasters on the production floor to learn how to air roast along with the art of home brewing and pour-overs.

THELMA'S KITCHEN

Can't afford lunch? Pay with service.

No one leaves hungry at Thelma's Kitchen.
This one-of-a-kind café in Kansas City's inner city is designed to bring people from all walks of life together. Customers are encouraged to pay what they can. Some give the minimum of $2 a meal. Most pay the normal $7 to $10 cost of lunch. Others throw in extra money to pay it forward. All the extra money collected turns into tokens, which are put aside and given to those who can't afford to buy lunch that day. Another way the poor can pay is through service. In exchange for a free meal, they can do a half hour of chores such as washing the dishes, bussing the tables, and cleaning the floors.

The idea of a community kitchen came from the mind of Thelma Gardner. For more than 30 years, she and her husband, Father Alexii Altschul, fed the poor and hungry in Kansas City's inner city. They ran a food pantry and served weekly meals, offering comfort food like Thelma's fried chicken, which received rave reviews. She helped thousands of people up until her death in 2012. In 2018, a Christian organization called Reconciliation Services opened a community café and named it Thelma's Kitchen in her honor. They put it on the first floor to their 100-year-old building at 31st and Troost. It was once an old candy store, but a different type of sweet is served there now: hope, love, and friendship.

Oh, and don't forget the great-tasting food. Thelma's Kitchen only serves lunch from 11 a.m. until 2 p.m., and every customer gets a four-course meal: soup, salad, entrée, and dessert. The food is prepared by a trained chef, and it's delicious. Customers can also get a vegan or gluten-free option if they so desire. Lunch is served

Top left: *You can eat your meal at the restaurant or take it to go.*

Bottom left: *Monetary donations are turned into tokens and given to those who can't afford a meal.*

Top center: *A mural of Thelma with a halo around her head symbolizes her kindness and generosity.*

Bottom center: *During the pandemic, they sold boxed lunches to the public.*

Right: *Thelma and her husband, Alexii. All images courtesy Thelma's Kitchen*

cafeteria-style at the front counter. After getting your tray, you're encouraged to sit with a stranger. Talk to them. With conversation, Thelma's Kitchen hopes to build a renewed sense of pride in this community. They want to tear down the walls of social isolation and bring people from all walks of life together through food.

3101 Troost Ave., Kansas City, MO, 816-931-4751
thelmaskitchen.org

> **It takes 16 volunteers a day to keep Thelma's Kitchen running. Many work a 90-minute shift one day a week. They are also encouraged to eat with customers to foster community.**

VIVILORE

A taste of elegance with a side of art

Before becoming the home of one of the most sought-after dining experiences in the metro area, Vivilore's brick building was an actual home. It was built more than 100-years ago, and several families lived there until 1949, when the son of Independence mayor Roger T. Sermon and his life partner, Mitch Anderson, bought it. They were one of the area's first openly gay couples, and they turned the house into the most exclusive interior design firms in all of Kansas City. People would dress up before visiting the Sermon & Anderson showroom. The couple lived and worked out of the building for more than 30 years, and they both died in the 1980s. The building then sat empty for more than three decades.

Fast-forward to 2010. Brother-sister duo Cindy Foster and Whit Ross drove past the beautiful structure one day and decided to buy it. It was in bad shape, and it took them two years to repair it. Wanting to create something truly special, they put a restaurant on the first floor and turned the top two floors into a gift shop. They sell unique artwork, sculptures, jewelry, antiques, and knickknacks. But the real focus is on the food. Whit is a classically trained chef and once ran the kitchen on the Missouri River Queen riverboat. His menu is focused on classic American cuisine, and they serve very large portions. Some of their best sellers include the grilled bone-in lamb chops, New Zealand rack of lamb, French Cut ribeye, and Pacific Coast wild salmon. To ensure quality seafood, Whit hired a chef from the Hamptons, and they now offer new seafood weekly.

As for the name Vivilore, it's the title of a female empowerment book written in 1900 by Dr. Mary Ried Melendy. It means "life story" in Latin. Before buying the building, Cindy

Left: *Every floor features rooms decorated with paintings, statues, and other works of art that are all for sale.*

Top right: *Every dish exudes elegance, and you are encouraged to take your time and enjoy the experience.*

Bottom right: *Owners Whit Ross and Cindy Foster. Courtesy Roy Inman*

and her friends often discussed the book over lunch and called themselves the "Vivilore ladies." When it came time to name the restaurant, she decided Vivilore was the perfect name.

Demand to eat here is so high that they recommend making a reservation. Every guest gets up to two hours to enjoy the experience, and by melding artwork with tasty food, Cindy and Whit have created a family-friendly, fine-dining destination.

10815 E Winner Rd., Independence, MO, 816-836-2222
vivilore.com

During the warmer months, many eat outside in a beautiful courtyard filled with statues and manicured bushes. Whit lives in a cottage on the grounds and also works as the decorator and gardener.

THE UPPER CRUST

A slice of buttery deliciousness in every bite

As kids growing up in central Kansas, Jan and her sister, Elaine, ate pie all the time. Their mother and grandmother made it from scratch for every family gathering. When the sisters grew older and moved to Kansas City, they tried but couldn't find a good homemade pie. All the pies they found for sale were made by machines with Crisco crust and canned filling. They tasted bland, not like the pies of their childhood.

Jan and Elaine dreamed of opening a pie business, but they were busy working other jobs and raising kids. In 2006, their mother volunteered to drive in with her family recipes to help them get started. The sisters rented a booth at the Overland Park Farmers Market and set 100 pies out on the table. They sold every single one of them. Demand grew overnight, and a few months later, they rented a space in Westport to make more of them. Within a few years they outgrew that space as well. In 2011, they moved their operation to downtown Overland Park and have been there ever since.

Over the past decade, they've made close to 25 different types of pies, everything from traditional apple to cherry, peach, lemon, coconut meringue, and bumbleberry, which is a combination of apple, blackberry, blueberry, and raspberry. The crust is 100-percent homemade and made with a lot of butter. It's flaky and literally melts in your mouth. While many of the recipes have been handed down from their family, others come from their own experimentation as they work to make traditional recipes even better.

The sisters spend two days a week making the pies and four days selling them. They typically sell around 100 pies a week, though during the holidays they've been known to sell as many

Top left: *A rack of homemade pies greets you when you walk in the door.*

Bottom left: *A worker tops lemon pies fresh out of the oven with homemade meringue.*

Top right: *Owners Jan Knobel and Elaine Van Buskirk. Courtesy The Upper Crust*

Bottom right: *Add a scoop of ice cream to your slice of pie.*

as 800 pies! They went into the business without a plan, trusting their pies would be good enough to sell, and it's worked out just fine. They've discovered people really love a good slice of pie because, as Jan says, "pie makes people happy, and we need happiness in our lives right now."

7943 Santa Fe Dr., Overland Park, KS, 913-642-2999
uppercrustpiebakery.com

> **Besides pie, you can also buy some cute kitchen knickknacks for your home like cloth napkins, plates, and aprons.**

OLD SHAWNEE PIZZA

The oldest business in Shawnee still serving slices

Before opening Old Shawnee Pizza, owner Joe Walker sold insurance.

The Moline, Kansas, native moved to Kansas City after his time in the Navy to start a new life. He met his wife, married, had three children, and sold insurance to pay the bills. Only he wasn't making enough money to pay the bills. His sister's husband, Dick Ryan, had opened a pizza restaurant called Pizza Shoppe, and in 1969, he asked Joe to franchise. Joe went to his dad and asked for a $5,000 loan. With that money, he opened his first pizza parlor.

Joe converted an old house in Shawnee into a Pizza Shoppe. He didn't know anything about the restaurant business, so he spent many nights sleeping in a cot in the basement and worked long hours to make his new venture a success. His hard work paid off, and his Pizza Shoppe became a favorite for many. Wanting a bigger building for the growing crowds, he bought the lot across the street and in 1985, built a new restaurant. It remained a Pizza Shoppe until 2003, when Joe parted ways with his brother-in-law. He renamed his restaurant Old Shawnee Pizza and modified the recipes slightly—not only for legal reasons but also to make his food taste even better. In 2012, Joe opened a second location in Lenexa.

What sets Old Shawnee Pizza apart is its cracker crust. They make it fresh everyday by fermenting a dry dough for 24 hours,

Dick Ryan's Pizza Shoppe franchise is still around today with dozens scattered around the metro area. While the cracker pizza crust is similar, their garlic salad dressing is a different color. Instead of being green, it's pink!

Top left: *Owner Joe Walker. Courtesy Old Shawnee Pizza*

Bottom left: *Step back into the 1980s when you walk into their Shawnee store.*

Top center: *The crab Rangoon pizza is well known on social media and shipped all over the country. Courtesy Old Shawnee Pizza*

Bottom center: *Don't forget a salad topped with their colorful green garlic salad dressing. Courtesy Old Shawnee Pizza*

Right: *The cracker crust helps these pizzas rise above the rest. Courtesy Old Shawnee Pizza*

rolling it into balls, and flattening them in a rolling machine. The result is a thin, crispy, mouthwatering crust that flakes with every bite. Another favorite is the house salad with garlic dressing. It's bright green and adds a great flavor. They also sell pastas and sandwiches, but their specialty remains pizza. One of their creations, the Crab Rangoon pizza, went viral with more than 20-million views online. People from both coasts have had it shipped to them!

Joe's pizza legacy remains in the family as his son, William, and daughter, Lisa, now run the stores. Joe's philosophy has always been that if you consistently put out a quality product, you'll be fine. By doing this, they hope to remain the favorite pizza joint for many families.

6000 Rogers Rd., Shawnee, KS, 913-631-5716
shawneepizza.com

Christopher Elbow Chocolates
Courtesy Christopher Elbow Chocolates

RESTAURANTS A-Z

Affäre, 2
1911 Main St., Kansas City, MO

AIXOIS Bistro, 96
251 E 55th St., Kansas City, MO

André's Confiserie Suisse, 10
5018 Main St., Kansas City, MO

Anthony's Restaurant & Lounge, 114
701 Grand Boulevard, Kansas City, MO

The Antler Room, 32
2506 Holmes St., Kansas City, MO

Arthur Bryant's, 52
1727 Brooklyn Ave., Kansas City, MO

Bamboo Penny's, 94
5270 W 116th Pl., Leawood, KS

Bistro 303/The Peacock, 76
303 Westport Rd., Kansas City, MO

Bo Ling's, 158
8973 Metcalf Ave., Overland Park, KS

Bonito Michoacán, 128
1150 Minnesota Ave., Kansas City, KS

Boulevard Brewing Tours & Recreation Center, 86
2534 Madison St., Kansas City, MO

Brew Lab, 8
7925 Marty St., Overland Park, KS

Browne's Irish Marketplace, 90
3300 Pennsylvania Ave., Kansas City, MO

Café Cà Phê, 130
916 E 5th St., Kansas City, MO

Café Gratitude, 110
333 Southwest Blvd., Kansas City, MO

Cardboard Corner Café, 66
9240 Metcalf Ave., Overland Park, KS

Chappell's Restaurant and Sports Museum, 64
323 Armour Rd., North Kansas City, MO

Chicken N Pickle, 120
1761 Burlington St., North Kansas City, MO

Christine's Firehouse, 136
220 E 20th Ave., North Kansas City, MO

Christopher Elbow Chocolates, 60
1819 McGee St., Kansas City, MO

Christy's Tasty Queen, 6
1405 S 55th St., Kansas City, KS

City Market, 106
20 E 5th St., Kansas City, MO

The Classic Cup Café, 144
301 W 47th St., Kansas City, MO

Joe's Kansas City, 46
3002 W 47th Ave., Kansas
City, KS

Jones BBQ, 104
6706 Kaw Dr., Kansas City, KS

Kelly's Westport Inn, 100
500 Westport Rd., Kansas
City, MO

Le Fou Frog, 88
400 E 5th St., Kansas City,
MO

Lenexa Public Market, 12
8750 Penrose Ln., Lenexa, KS

Local Pig + Pigwich, 92
20 E 5th St., Kansas City, MO

Lonnie's Reno Club, 142
1111 Grand Blvd., Kansas
City, MO

The Majestic Restaurant, 150
931 Broadway Blvd., Kansas
City, MO

Messenger Coffee/Ibis
Bakery, 98
1624 Grand St., Kansas City,
MO

Mugs Up, 124
700 E 23rd St. S,
Independence, MO

Neighborhood Café, 16
104 SE Third St., Lee's
Summit, MO

New Theatre &
Restaurant, 36
9929 Foster, Overland Park,
KS

Old Shawnee Pizza, 172
6000 Rogers Rd., Shawnee,
KS

The Peanut, 42
5000 Main St., Kansas City,
MO

Piropos, 102
4141 N Mulberry Dr., Kansas
City, MO

Ponak's, 74
2856 Southwest Blvd., Kansas
City, MO

The Quaff, 162
1010 Broadway Blvd., Kansas
City, MO

The Roasterie, 164
1204 W 27th St., Kansas City,
MO

Rozzelle Court at the
Nelson-Atkins Museum, 112
4525 Oak St., Kansas City,
MO

Ruby Jean's Juicery, 126
3000 Troost Ave., Kansas City,
MO

The Savoy at 21c, 58
219 W 9th St., Kansas City,
MO

The Ship, 82
1221 Union Ave., Kansas City,
MO

SPIN! Pizza, 116
6541 W 119th St., Overland
Park, KS

Strang Hall, 152
7313 W 80th St., Overland
Park, KS

Stroud's, 132
5410 NE Oak Ridge Dr.,
Kansas City, MO

Sylas and Maddy's Homemade Ice Cream, 138
11925 Strang Line Rd., Olathe, KS

Taps on Main, 140
1715 Main St., Kansas City, MO

Thelma's Kitchen, 166
3101 Troost Ave., Kansas City, MO

Third Street Social, 24
123 SE Third St., Lee's Summit, MO

Tom's Town, 22
Main St., Kansas City, MO

The Town Company, 62
1228 Baltimore Ave., Kansas City, MO

Town Topic, 108
2021 Broadway Blvd., Kansas City, MO

The Upper Crust, 170
7943 Santa Fe Dr., Overland Park, KS

V's Italiano Ristorante, 134
10819 E Hwy. 40, Independence, MO

Vivilore, 168
10815 E Winner Rd., Independence, MO,

Westport Flea Market, 30
817 Westport Rd., Kansas City, MO

Woodyard Bar-B-Que, 34
3001 Merriam Ln., Merriam, KS

Joe's Kansas City
Courtesy Joe's Kansas City

APPENDIX

DOWNTOWN KANSAS CITY

WEST BOTTOMS

EAST BOTTOMS

CROSSROADS

MIDTOWN-WESTPORT

THE PLAZA

BROOKSIDE

KANSAS CITY SOUTH

KANSAS CITY NORTH

NORTH KANSAS CITY, MO

Chappell's Restaurant and
   Sports Museum, 64
Chicken N Pickle, 120
Christine's Firehouse, 136
Iron District, 156

RIVERSIDE, MO

The Corner Café, 80

INDEPENDENCE, MO

Clinton's Soda Fountain, 154
Courthouse Exchange, 28
Dixon's Famous Chili, 70
Mugs Up, 124
V's Italiano Ristorante, 134
Vivilore, 168

LEE'S SUMMIT, MO

Neighborhood Café, 16
Third Street Social, 24

MARTIN CITY, MO

Jack Stack Barbecue, 84
Jess and Jim's Steakhouse, 4

KANSAS CITY, KS

Bonito Michoacán, 128
Christy's Tasty Queen, 6
Fritz's Railroad Restaurant, 26
Joe's Kansas City, 46
Jones BBQ, 104
Woodyard Bar-B-Que, 34

LEAWOOD, KS

Bamboo Penny's, 94

LENEXA, KS

Lenexa Public Market, 12

MISSION, KS

Fluffy Fresh Donuts, 48

OVERLAND PARK, KS

Bo Ling's, 158
Brew Lab, 8
Cardboard Corner Cafe, 66
The Golden Scoop, 72
New Theatre & Restaurant, 36
SPIN! Pizza, 116
Strang Hall, 152
The Upper Crust, 170

OLATHE, KS

Sylas and Maddy's Homemade
   Ice Cream, 138

SHAWNEE, KS

Old Shawnee Pizza, 172